Werner Krüger

Business Grammar Intermediate

Business Grammar Intermediate wurde geplant und entwickelt von der Verlagsredaktion der Cornelsen und Oxford University Press GmbH, Berlin.

Verfasser:	Werner Krüger, Immenstaad
Verlagsredaktion:	James Austin M.A., Rosalind Beavis B.A.
Layout/Herstellung:	Sabine Trittin

Erhältlich sind auch:	Business Grammar Elementary (Best.-Nr. 27465)
	Business Vocabulary Elementary (Best.-Nr. 27520)
	Business Vocabulary Intermediate (Best.-Nr. 27538)
	Business Grammar and Vocabulary (Best.-Nr. 24210)

1. Auflage

5.	4.	3.	2.	1.	Die letzten Ziffern bezeichnen Zahl
99	98	97	96	95	und Jahr des Druckes.

Alle Drucke dieser Auflage können, weil untereinander unverändert, im Unterricht nebeneinander verwendet werden.

Bestellnummer 27473

© 1995 Cornelsen & Oxford University Press GmbH, Berlin.

Das Werk und seine Teile sind urheberrechtlich geschützt. Jede Verwertung in anderen als den gesetzlich zugelassenen Fällen bedarf deshalb der vorherigen schriftlichen Einwilligung des Verlages.

ISBN 3-8109-2747-3

Druck:	Saladruck
Weiterverarbeitung:	Hensch
Vertrieb:	Cornelsen Verlag, Berlin

Gedruckt auf chlorfrei gebleichtem Papier ohne Dioxinbelastung der Gewässer.

Vorwort

Sie haben sich für dieses Buch entschieden, weil Sie wissen, daß nicht allein Ihre, sondern die Hauptschwäche eines jeden Sprachenlernenden darin liegt, die grammatische Unsicherheit zu beseitigen / besiegen.

Business Grammar Intermediate ist sowohl ein Grammatik- als auch ein Übungsbuch. Es ist bestimmt für Lernende aller Altersstufen, die ihre sprachlichen Grundkenntnisse durch kaufmännisches Englisch, ob allein oder mit anderen, erweitern wollen.

Business Grammar Intermediate ist ein Aufgaben- und Arbeitsbuch. Ein grammatisches Problem wird schrittweise erklärt, und jeder Erklärung folgt das entsprechende Übungsmaterial. Die Übungen sind in ihrem Schwierigkeitsgrad sorgfältig aufeinander abgestimmt. Alle Beispiel- und Übungssätze stammen aus dem sprachlichen Umfeld des Business English. Die Lösungen können Sie im beiliegenden Schlüssel nachschlagen.

In drei Schritten werden Sie zu Erfolg kommen:

1. Schritt:	Darstellung und Erklärung des grammatischen Problems	*Einsicht in die Problematik und Verstehen*
2. Schritt:	Schematische Übungen	*Vertiefen und Festigen*
3. Schritt:	Freie Übungen	*Anwendung durch Rückgriff auf Einsicht und Festigung*

Vor dem Erfolg steht die Arbeit. Es gibt viel zu tun.
Also packen wir's an!

Berlin, im Juli 1995   Werner Krüger

Inhalt

		Seite
1	**Die Adverbien**	5
2	**Die Indirekte Rede**	23
3	**Das Passiv**	38
4	**Die Zeiten**	53
5	**Die Konditionalsätze (if-Sätze)**	75
6	**Die modalen Hilfsverben**	87
7	**Das Gerundium**	108
8	**Das Partizip**	124
9	**Der Infinitiv**	137

Die Adverbien

Einführung

- Adjektive beschreiben ein Substantiv näher. Sie antworten auf die Frage: Was für ein? z.b. ein *guter* Rat.

- Adverbien (auch adverbiale Bestimmungen) bezeichnen die äußeren Umstände, unter denen etwas geschieht:

Adverbien des Ortes	wo, woher, wohin	*here, there*
der Zeit	wann, seit/bis wann	*always, today, yesterday*
der Art und Weise	wie (wird etwas getan)	*slowly, easily*

- Im Deutschen benutzt man für Adjektive und Adverbien die gleichen Formen, im Englischen wird in den meisten Fällen ein *-ly* an den Wortstamm angehängt.

- Da Adverbien an verschiedenen Stellen eines Satzes (bzw. Haupt- und Nebensatzes) stehen können oder müssen, teilen wir sie ein in:

  - **Bestimmte Adverbien**
    des Ortes: *here, there*
    der bestimmten Zeit: *yesterday, today*

  - **Unbestimmte Adverbien**
    der Art und Weise: *quickly, politely*
    der unbestimmten Zeit: *already, frequently*

Die Stellung der Adverbien

- Bestimmte Adverbien (und adverbiale Bestimmungen) stehen am Anfang oder Schluß eines Satzes, das sind die Stellen, wo sie am meisten Gewicht haben. (Denken Sie an das Beispiel einer Wippe auf dem Kinderspielplatz: ganz außen wirkt das Gewicht am meisten.)

  The meeting began *two hours ago*.
  In London you will find many of our branches.

Übung 1

Setzen Sie das Adverb (bzw. die adverbiale Bestimmung) an die richtige Stelle. Manchmal ist mehr als eine Lösung richtig.

BEISPIEL (tomorrow) Mr Reade, the Managing Director of Empire Office Furniture Ltd is going to meet Mrs Brown.
Tomorrow Mr Reade ... is going to meet Mrs Brown.
oder: *Mr Reade ... is going to meet Mrs Brown tomorrow.*

1 (since 1920) Empire Office Furniture Ltd has been in business.
2 (in Wales) The company has a subsidiary.
3 (from their headquarters) They manage all their branches.
4 (in the early eighties) Mr Reade thought he could cover the whole of the domestic market.
5 (during the recession) The workforce was gradually reduced.
6 (during the last five years) Twenty per cent of all office workers have been made redundant.
7 (on the managerial level) A lot of changes had to be made, too.
8 (at the Annual General Meeting) The atmosphere was rather cool.
9 (by the end of the year) Things have changed now. The company will have expanded considerably.
10 (in the next decade) Competition from the Far East will increase.
11 (every week) There is a board meeting.
12 (this morning) The agenda was fixed.
13 (today) Mr Reade's secretary has worked very hard.
14 (by six o'clock) She hopes to finish her work.

Die Stellung der Adverbien

- Unbestimmte Adverbien stehen in einfachen Zeiten (die nur mit einem Verb gebildet werden) zwischen Subjekt und Prädikat (d.h. vor dem Verb):

    We *seldom* open an account with new customers.

Übung 2

Setzen Sie die unbestimmten Adverbien an die richtige Stelle.

BEISPIEL (never) He forgets his secretary's birthday.
He never forgets his secretary's birthday.

1 (politely) Our receptionist invites guests to have a cup of tea or coffee.
2 (always) We offer important customers the use of a company car.
3 (urgently) We requested the completion of the order.
4 (frequently) They tried to sell their management expertise abroad.
5 (certainly) He thinks that the Far East will provide us with vast new markets.
6 (regularly) They send updated address lists to the local distributors.
7 (reluctantly) Mr Reade agreed to bear the cost of advertising.
8 (clearly) Your references show me that you have expert knowledge in the field.
9 (wisely) They invited women directors on to the board.
10 (always) Our boss consults the marketing team before taking a decision.
11 (patiently) He explained how to fill in the form.
12 (finally) They found a compromise.
13 (impatiently) Mr Reade asked where the plans were.
14 (immediately) Tom admitted that he had mislaid the papers.
15 (kindly) Penny offered her help to find them.

Die Stellung der Adverbien

- Unbestimmte Adverbien (Adverbien der Art und Weise und Adverbien der unbestimmten Zeit) stehen in zusammengesetzten Zeiten (d.h. Zeiten, die mit mehr als nur einem Verb gebildet werden) nach dem ersten Hilfsverb:

    They have *quietly* gone into liquidation.

- Unbestimmte Adverbien stehen nach einer Form von *to be*:

    Our receptionist is *always* charming.

Übung 3

Setzen Sie die gegebenen Adverbien an die richtige Stelle. Bei manchen Sätzen gibt es mehrere mögliche Lösungen.

BEISPIEL (quietly) He had left the firm before the end of the year.
He had quietly left the firm before the end of the year.

1 (always) Tom, the junior clerk, is the first person to collect the mail from the postroom in the morning.
2 (carefully) He has set aside all the envelopes marked PERSONAL, CONFIDENTIAL, or PRIVATE.
3 (easily) These letters are dealt with.
4 (sometimes) Tom is a little late for work.
5 (considerably) A letter-opening machine would speed up the task of opening the envelopes.
6 (always) But there is Penny, the typist, who can help.
7 (always) Tom is well-liked at the office: he is friendly and polite.
8 (always) A circulation slip is attached to those letters which have several addressees.
9 (clearly) Every letter should be stamped with a date stamp.
10 (carefully) Tom has sorted the correspondence. It didn't take long today.
11 (quickly) Having done the morning post, the junior clerk usually finds time for a cup of tea.
12 (sometimes) A letter is addressed to more than one person.

Die Stellung der Adverbien

- Unbestimmte Adverbien können bei starker Hervorhebung auch am Anfang oder am Ende eines Satzes stehen:

  Fortunately we closed our account with them.
  They read the annual report *carefully*.

Übung 4

Entscheiden Sie, welchen Satzteil Sie betonen wollen, und setzen Sie je ein Adverb bzw. eine adverbiale Bestimmung an die richtige Stelle. Es gibt oft mehrere Lösungen.

easily – certainly – perhaps – nervously – wisely – carefully – more punctually – willingly – fortunately – often – already – always

1. She returned in time for the meeting.
2. He has shouted at him twice this morning.
3. They will try to make the best of it.
4. The senior clerk told him to start work.
5. Mr Reade has read every paragraph of the contract.
6. It will be finished by the end of the month.
7. You can find the letter in the filing cabinet.
8. He has thrown it into the waste-paper basket.
9. She is looking for the missing file.
10. Tom is willing to do Penny a favour.
11. Mrs Jenkins prefers the telephone to a memo.
12. They accepted our suggestions.

Die Bildung der abgeleiteten Adverbien

Bei der Rechtschreibung und Bildung einiger Adverbien muß man aufpassen.

- Abgeleitete Adverbien *(quietly, frequently, surprisingly)* bildet man einfach durch das Anhängen von *-ly:*

  > quiet → *quietly*

- Manchmal allerdings verändert sich die Rechtschreibung:
  - *-le* fällt aus nach vorausgehenden Konsonanten:

    > possible → *possibly*

  - stummes *-e* fällt aus bei *due* und *true*:

    > due → *duly*

  - *-y* nach Mitlaut wird zu *i*:

    > happy → *happily*

- Wörter auf *-ly* können kein zweites *-ly* nehmen, sondern werden umschrieben:

  > friendly → *in a friendly way*

- Andere müssen grundsätzlich umschrieben werden:

  > difficult → *with difficulty*

- Die meisten Adjektive auf *-ic* fügen *-ally* an:

  > democratic → *democratically*

  aber public → *publicly*

- Das Adjektiv *good* wird zum Adverb *well*:

  | good → well |

  A *good* typist types *well*.

- Einige Adjektive und Adverbien haben die gleiche Form und die gleiche Bedeutung. Hierzu gehören Zeitbestimmungen wie *early, daily, weekly, monthly*. Ferner *enough, far, fast, hard, little, long* und *much*.

  The newspapers come *daily*. (Adverb)
  We have not subscribed to a *daily* paper. (Adjektiv)
  A *fast* (Adjektiv) runner runs *fast* (Adverb).

- Auch einige Formen des Komparativs und Superlativs bilden keine gesonderten Adverbialformen: *better, best, less, least, worse, worst*.

Übung 5

Bilden Sie Adverbien.

BEISPIEL They ... (willing) agreed to postpone payment because of the strike.
They willingly agreed to postpone payment because of the strike.

1. He said he would ... (full) support him in this matter.
2. They ... (ready) sent us their latest catalogue.
3. I was ... (confidential) approached by the personnel manager before he sacked Mr Whitaker.
4. He had ... (complete) forgotten the appointment and apologized.
5. Whoever the customer might be, he must be greeted ... (friendly).
6. She ... (polite) asked whether she could have a day off.
7. The strike is ... (possible) to blame for this.
8. He ... (decided) rejected any demands for further discounts.
9. He works ... (good) and to the full satisfaction of his line manager.
10. His knowledge of English is ... (remarkable) good.
11. They ... (due) apologized for forgetting to send the documents.
12. ... (strict) speaking it does not quite correspond to the draft contract.

Die Aufgabe der Adverbien der Art und Weise

- Die Adverbien der Art und Weise drücken aus, **wie** etwas getan wird. Man erfragt sie also mit: Wie tut jemand etwas? Wie wurde etwas getan? usw. Das Verb muß auch ein Tun ausdrücken, wie arbeiten, kommen, schreiben usw. Nur solche Verben nehmen ein Adverb auf *-ly*.

She can type accurately and quickly.
He speaks slowly and clearly.

Übung 6

Im ersten Satz finden Sie die Eigenschaft einer Person angegeben (Adjektiv). Im zweiten sollen Sie einsetzen, wie diese Person etwas tut (Adverb).

BEISPIEL   He is a brilliant translator. He can translate ..., particularly from French into English.
He can translate brilliantly, particularly ...

1 Mary is an accurate clerk. She always does her work ... .
2 We have a good filing clerk. She will look after the files ... .
3 Penny is very happy today. It is her birthday. She is smiling ... at everybody.
4 Mrs Jenkins is a very patient negotiator. She can negotiate ... for hours.
5 She is fluent in French. She speaks French ... .
6 He is a serious young man. Whatever he does, he does it ... .
7 A good receptionist must be friendly. She must always treat visitors ... .
8 It is a comfortable armchair. You can sit very ... in it.
9 The entire stock was destroyed by the fire. The fire destroyed the stock ... .
10 They are very careless filing clerks. They ... mislay documents and then we spend hours looking for them.
11 Susan is a very kind person. She ... agreed to help me when I needed advice.
12 Mr Reade is a slow and careful driver. He always drives ... and ... .

Übung 7

Vervollständigen Sie die Sätze mit einem Adverb bzw. Adjektiv.

BEISPIEL   They ... (spontaneous) accepted the offer.
They spontaneously accepted the offer.

1. Our junior clerk is an ... (intelligent) boy.
2. The goods arrived ... (punctual) before Easter.
3. The decision was ... (quick) made.
4. They always treat candidates ... (polite).
5. It was an ... (unexpected) visit.
6. The auditor checked all their books ... (thorough).
7. You can rely on him, he is a ... (trustworthy) man.
8. This is a ... (complete) list of last month sales.
9. The sales rep arrived ... (unexpected) and Mr Reade was not in.
10. Penny asked Mr Reade for a rise and he made her a ... (generous) offer.
11. In her department most decisions are made ... (democratic).
12. Sue is ... (careful) with her budget and never overspends.

Das Adjektiv nach Verben, die keine Tätigkeit ausdrücken

◆ Es gibt auch Verben, die keine Tätigkeit beschreiben und deshalb auch keine Adverbien auf *-ly* bilden. Solche Verben sind: *to be, to become, to stay, to seem, to look, to smell, to taste, to sound.*

She is quiet.	sein
He is becoming nervous.	werden
They look reliable.	aussehen
It sounds fine.	klingen

Übung 8

Vervollständigen Sie die Sätze mit dem passenden Adverb bzw. Adjektiv. Fragen Sie sich, ob das Verb ein Tun ausdrückt (dann Adverb auf -ly) oder nicht (dann Form ohne -ly).

BEISPIELE Mrs Jenkins sometimes dictates her letters too ... (quick).
Mrs Jenkins sometimes dictates her letters too quickly.
She is back at work and seems ... (fine) after her long illness.
She is back at work and seems fine after her long illness.

1. The new filing cabinet looks ... (fine).
2. They answered the enquiry ... (immediate).
3. He nearly lost his self-control, but seems ... (calm) now.
4. The new word processors were welcomed ... (enthusiastic).
5. The salesman became more and more ... (aggressive) on the phone.
6. Your representative said the new tea tasted ... (excellent).
7. She ... (careful) unplugged the machine before starting to clean it.
8. Mrs Jenkins, our sales manager, remains ... (polite) in any situation.
9. They looked ... (sad) when they heard about the branch being closed down.
10. Tom liked Penny at first sight but was not sure if the feeling was ... (mutual).

Was Adverbien näher bestimmen

♦ Adverbien können folgende Satzteile näher bestimmen:

ein Verb	They *reluctantly* accepted the terms.
ein Adjektiv	It is an *extremely* favourable offer.
ein anderes Adverb	The letter arrived *surprisingly* soon.
einen ganzen Satz	*Perhaps* we should agree to his terms.

Übung 9

Vervollständigen Sie die Sätze mit einem Adverb bzw. Adjektiv.

BEISPIEL   They are . . . . (extreme, generous)
They are extremely generous.

1   They are all . . . . . . after a day like this. (terrible, tired)
2   He is . . . bad-tempered today. (real)
3   She will . . . not agree to our suggestion. (probable)
4   We are . . . . . . with new customers. (particular, careful)
5   Sometimes he becomes . . . . (extreme, irritable)
6   As far as fair competition is concerned, she is . . . . (high, sensitive)
7   . . . you should try to find a new supplier . . . . (perhaps, immediate)
8   She . . . offered her a seat. (kind)

Übung 10

Setzen Sie das gleiche Wort in Form und Funktion eines Adverbs, eines Adjektivs zu einem Substantiv oder eines Adjektivs zu einem Verb, das keine Tätigkeit ausdrückt, ein.

BEISPIEL   due
Payment is *due* after two weeks.
They have *duly* offered compensation for the damage.
They will get payment in *due* course.

1   particular
Penny had a hard time working for Empire Office Furniture Ltd, . . . when she was new.
She had to listen to the advice of the senior clerk with . . . attention.
From time to time she asked the same thing about a . . . piece of office practice twice.
She seemed . . . good at her job from the very first day.
2   remarkable
It is quite a . . . computer program – it even corrects spelling mistakes.
Mr Reade was . . . patient with him.
Last year's turnover was . . . . It was nearly 23% up on the previous year.

3   usual
    ... compliment slips are small pieces of paper which have brief details of the company and the words "with compliments" on them.
    They are the ... way of sending a short message instead of, say, a covering letter accompanying catalogues and price lists and they might have the sender's signature on them.
    In Penny's company memos are ... used for internal messages.
    On a memo pad you ... find the words: *Date, To, From* and *Subject.*

4   high
    A general clerk is not a ... specialized clerical worker.
    But it is more and more difficult to find a job in times of computerization and ... unemployment.
    Selecting the right stationery seems to be extremely simple, but in fact it is ... complex.
    Finding the correct postal rates for various items to different destinations requires a ... degree of concentration.

5   general
    The sort of paper that is ... used for business correspondence is called bond paper.
    The size of paper ... used is A4 or A5.
    If you send a letter "... delivery" in the US, you send it to a particular post office, where the addressee can collect it.
    Over the last few years postal rates have gone up despite a ... decline in service.

6   safe
    Calculators, staplers and other items should not be left lying about, they must be put in a ... place.
    Flammable liquids like thinners or spirit for spirit duplicators must be stored ... as they are a fire hazard.
    A ... place for documents is a filing cabinet.

7   main
    The ... advantage with airmail letters is that they reach their destinations fast.
    No-carbon-required paper is widely used – ... to save time.
    Companies try to increase their turnover by making ordering easy for customers, ... by providing reply-paid envelopes (Business Reply Service).

Die Reihenfolge der Adverbien im Satz

- Wenn mehrere Adverbien verschiedener Art zusammentreffen, gilt normalerweise folgende Anordnung:

  Art und Weise – Ort – Zeit

  My boss spoke to me *angrily in the meeting yesterday*.

  > **Merke:** A–O–Z im Alphabet

  Genauere Bestimmungen stehen vor allgemeineren:

  We met him at *Meeting Point B in the entrance hall*.

Übung 11

Setzen Sie die Adverbien an die richtige Stelle. Es gibt oft mehrere richtige Lösungen.

1. We are going (next week, to the export fair, certainly)
2. We will stay (for the rest of the week, there, probably)
3. Mr Reade likes a cup of tea (in the morning, early)
4. I'm sorry, but my bus was (this morning, late)
5. You can meet Mr Reade (every afternoon, at our stand, between three and four o'clock)
6. I talked to him (yesterday, in his office)
7. He was (on the continent, last year, several times)
8. She spends most of her time (in the design room, at her computer)
9. We will meet him (tomorrow morning, at the airport, at 9.15 a.m.)
10. He is preparing to go (already, home)
11. We will get a lot of orders and find new customers (at the trade fair, next month, in London)
12. He finds that demand exceeds supply (often, above all before Christmas, in the high-street branches)
13. He comes (in the morning, to the office, before nine, never)
14. We have our Christmas dinner (always, at the five-star hotel, in town)

Adverbien mit Doppelformen

- Einige Adverbien haben eine Form mit *-ly* und eine ohne *-ly*, wobei die Bedeutungen verschieden sind. Meistens wird die Form auf *-ly* in übertragenem Sinne gebraucht.

late	spät	He turned up *late* and apologized.
lately	vor kurzem	We haven't had any news from them *lately*.
just	gerade, eben	The daily post has *just* come in.
justly	berechtigt	He was *justly* blamed for interfering.
hard	schwer, stark	Every Friday we work *hard* to get everything done before the weekend.
hardly	kaum	She is always present but *hardly* works.

Übung 12

Setzen Sie eins von den beiden angegebenen Adverbien in die Lücken ein.

1. late/lately
   We have not had any difficulties with them . . . .
2. hard/hardly
   It was so much that we could . . . finish it.
3. late/lately
   We have received a lot of complaints . . . about this type of machine.
4. just/justly
   It has . . . been confirmed that we can claim compensation.
5. late/lately
   I'm afraid we are . . . sending out our catalogues this year.
6. just/justly
   Why did you tell him . . . before his holidays?
7. hard/hardly
   Filing all those letters can . . . be done before five p.m.
8. late/lately
   They have been paying us . . . for some time now.

Im Deutschen Adverbien, im Englischen Verben

♦ Einige deutsche Adverbien werden oft durch Verben ausgedrückt. (Zunehmend jedoch bürgern sich im modernen Englisch Formen ein wie *hopefully, supposedly, presumably* usw.)

hoffentlich	*We hope to* get the order.
lieber	*They prefer to* pay in cash.
vermutlich	*We suppose (presume)* they will accept our terms of trade.
leider	*I'm sorry (I'm afraid)* he is not in his office at the moment.
zufällig	We *happened to* meet him at the fair.
weiter, dauernd	*They continue to* expand in the UK market.
anscheinend	Toddler Toys *seem to* be a very successful company.

Übung 13

Übersetzen Sie die deutsch vorgegebenen Adverbien ins Englische.

BEISPIEL (leider) this size is not in stock.
I'm afraid this size is not in stock.

1 (zufällig) They met in the dentist's waiting room.
2 (hoffentlich) They will get on with each other.
3 (anscheinend) They are young, have long hair and wear strange clothes but are good workers.
4 (weiter) They send us their latest price lists and catalogues.
5 (lieber) I meet him personally rather than just have a conversation on the phone.
6 (vermutlich) She will be in Paris when you come to see us.
7 (leider) I cannot pass on the details of our sales figures.
8 (lieber) He always stays at home at the weekends.
9 (hoffentlich) The goods in transport were sufficiently insured.
10 (anscheinend) Our new customer is a bulk buyer and should be treated very politely.

Zusammenfassende Übungen

Übung 14

Bilden Sie aus den gegebenen Satzteilen sinnvolle Sätze. Beachten Sie, daß die unterstrichenen Wörter Adverbien oder Adjektive sein können. Es gibt öfter mehrere richtige Lösungen.

BEISPIEL   He/obvious/had forgotten/the meeting
He had obviously forgotten the meeting.
or: *Obviously he had forgotten the meeting.*

1   found/they/our suggestions/unacceptable
2   the number of telex machines/steady/in modern offices/is decreasing
3   our budgeted sales performance/differs/from our real overall sales performance/slight
4   he/cut him short/angry
5   the morning/booked up/is/unfortunate/but/would be convenient/the early afternoon
6   high-street prices/because of the recession/sharp/falling/are
7   were answered/all our questions/clear
8   it has been/so far/a morning/terrible/busy
9   to cut a long story short/considerable/must improve/our sales figures
10 equal/essential/market research/in our firm/are regarded as/and sales promotion
11 must be solved/this problem/urgent
12 he thinks/always/field research/unnecessary/causes/expenses
13 he/pointed at the gap between the two lines/furious/on the graph
14 we ran short of our pocket models/before sales started/just
15 always/they are/in settling their accounts/punctual
16 produce/at a high cost/relative/they/them
17 deal/it was/a most profitable
18 we priced/our export models/from our models for the domestic market/independent
19 is easy/the cheap model/real/to handle
20 to be efficient/privatized enterprises/always/have not proved

Übung 15

Bilden Sie Sätze mit den Adverbien oder Adjektiven.

1 (complete) We would like to sign the contract but we do not ... agree to the terms of payment.
2 (considerable) Automation has resulted in ... higher productivity.
3 (strange) At first the story of the lost containers sounded ... .
4 (clear) Your contract of employment ... states what your responsibilities are.
5 (chaotic) The management structure of the company is not centralized, that's why working conditions are ... .
6 (brisk) When the recession is over there will be a ... demand for electrical consumer goods.
7 (surprising) The devaluation of the pound led to a ... fast recovery from the economic crisis.
8 (profitable) Going on an exchange programme can be very ... : one can really learn a lot.
9 (traditional) Team management is changing the ... concept of management.
10 (late) We haven't heard anything from them ... .
11 (hard) They say that there are some people in our company who ... work, but I can assure you that most of us work very ... .
12 (large) We have registered a ... increase in late deliveries this month.
13 (considerable) Our stand at the fair impressed them ... .
14 (complete) The idea was not a ... new one.
15 (high) He will need a ... degree of skill for the job.
16 (suspicious) They watched him ... from the gatehouse.
17 (bad) We have been informed that the machines were ... damaged during transport.
18 (impartial) The chairperson should preside over the meeting ... , but he/she has a casting vote if the meeting is divided on any one point.
19 (effective) Our new measures to reduce absenteeism ... will be introduced in all branches by the end of the year.
20 (economical) Our new spray guns are extremely ... because the paint waste has been reduced by 50 per cent.

Übung 16

Entscheiden Sie: Adjektiv und Adverb.

Insurance

Original[1] merchants and shipowners in Italy in the 12th century wanted to share their risks and so created the oldest branch of insurance: marine insurance. As fires frequent[2] destroyed parts of towns and cities, fire insurance companies were established in the 17th century. Life assurance followed later/more lately[3] and then accident insurance developed this century especially in the high[4] industrialised countries.

Today, third-party insurance is of particular[5] importance. It covers damages which the insured person (1st. party) inflicts on somebody else (3rd. party) and which are general[6] covered by the insurance company (2nd. party). The terms of the insurance can be very complicated. Often the small print in a proposal form is hard[7] understandable[8]. But there are some general principles every insurer and insured person has to keep to very strict[9].

The principle of "utmost good faith" demands that the insured person must honest[10] give the insurer all the details about the item he or she wants to insure. You can only insure against a risk that real[11] results in a loss if it occurs.

The "principle of indemnity" states that nobody is allowed to make a profit out of a loss. A policy holder can never be put in a better financial[12] position than he or she was in before the risk occurred. Sometimes people serious[13] think they can get more compensation by insuring with more than one insurance company.

The "principle of contribution" rules that each insurer only pays a percentage, so that the insured person is compensated for the exact[14] sum which he or she has lost.

An insured person will have his or her compensation considerable[15] scaled down in a case of underinsurance ("principle of averaging").

Die indirekte Rede

Einführung

- In der indirekten Rede wird wiedergegeben, was jemand gesagt hat.

  Sie fragte: „Wo wohnst du?"
  Sie fragte, wo ich wohne.

  He said, "I have talked to you on the phone."
  Er sagte: „Ich habe mit Ihnen telefoniert."

  He said that he had talked to me on the phone.
  Er sagte, daß er mit mir telefoniert hätte.

- Im Gegensatz zum Deutschen gibt es im Englischen keine Möglichkeitsform (Konjunktiv). Die Schwierigkeiten mit habe, hätte, sei, wäre, käme usw. entfallen also.

Die Befehlsform in der indirekten Rede

- Bei der Umsetzung der Befehlsform geben Sie den Befehl wieder, indem Sie *tell* (und *ask, advise, beg, command, encourage, forbid, urge, warn*) verwenden und den Infinitiv mit *to* folgen lassen:

  He said, "Settle this invoice immediately."
  He told me to settle the invoice immediately.

- Sie können aber auch das Verb *say* gebrauchen und mit *should* anschließen:

  He said I should settle the invoice immediately.

Übung 1

Benutzen Sie nun beide Formen, wenn Sie die indirekte Rede bilden.

BEISPIEL   Bring in the letters. (He told me)
He told me to bring in the letters.
He said I should bring in the letters.

1. Come to my office. (He asked me)
2. Write it without mistakes. (He urged her)
3. Hold it for me. (She asked me)
4. Despatch the goods promptly. (He urged us)
5. Offer bonuses to the office workers. (He advised me)
6. Increase the foremen's wages. (They advised Mr Reade)
7. Give reasons for your demand. (She urged him)
8. Improve canteen services. (They asked them)
9. Give us more detailed instructions. (We asked them)
10. Present an alternative. (He advised us)
11. Advertise in the local press. (They advised us)
12. Organize the workers into smaller teams. (He told me)
13. Introduce more automation. (They encouraged us)
14. Rationalize your filing system. (I advised them)
15. Train them better. (He urged us)
16. Spend more money on TV advertising. (He encouraged us)
17. Replace the old machinery as fast as possible. (He told them)
18. Build up a highly skilled workforce. (I encouraged them)

Die verneinte Befehlsform

♦ Die verneinte Befehlsform wird durch den verneinten Infinitiv wiedergegeben.

He said, "Don't do it again".
He asked me not to do it again.

Übung 2

Bilden Sie die indirekte Rede und verwenden Sie folgende Verben:

ask – order – warn – advise – beg – urge – request – encourage – forbid – tell

Die Personen, die die Anweisungen geben, sind in Klammern angegeben. Die Personalpronomen wie me, us, him, them müssen Sie diesmal selbst finden.

BEISPIEL   Don't reject the goods. (Mr Reade)
           Mr Reade told us not to reject the goods.

1. Don't keep me waiting again. (Mrs Jenkins)
2. Don't hesitate to accept the cheque. (Our accountant)
3. Don't go to him without being prepared. (Bill)
4. Don't do too much overtime. (Our shop steward)
5. Don't be too frank with him. (They)
6. Don't lose your temper with them. (She)
7. Don't turn her down just because of a few mistakes. (He)
8. Don't locate one department in two different places. (The architect)
9. Don't look for a new supplier too fast. (Our buyer)
10. Don't accept new conditions without Mrs Grant's agreement. (Susan)

Übung 3

Geben Sie die Anweisungen über den firmenüblichen Stil am Telefon an eine Kollegin weiter. Benutzen Sie einleitende Sätze wie:

She said we should, that we should never;
We were told (not, never) to usw.

BEISPIEL   Always have a message pad and a pen ready.
           She told us to always have a message pad and a pen ready.

1. Don't hold the receiver in the hand you write with.
2. Give your firm's name and be polite.
3. Use the caller's name when possible.
4. Don't keep callers waiting for a long time.

5 Do not argue, but be understanding if someone complains.
6 Never put any blame on one of the staff members.
7 Write down essential facts on your pad.
8 Read back names, figures and telephone numbers to avoid misunderstandings.
9 Offer to ring back if you cannot answer a question immediately.
10 Do not forget to offer help.
11 Take down as many details of a complaint as possible.
12 Apologize if you cannot offer immediate help.
13 Never give vague answers.
14 Reassure callers if they have a complaint.

Übung 4

In dieser Übung geht es um die Benutzung eines Laserdruckers.
Bilden Sie die indirekte Rede und benutzen Sie folgende Einleitungen:

They said we should … ;	We were told never to … ;
I learnt that we should never … ;	We were advised (not) to … ;
We were told (not) to … ;	We were warned not to …

BEISPIEL   Read all the instructions in the manual.
We were told to read all the instructions in the manual.
They said we should read all the instructions in the manual.

1 Unplug the printer before cleaning.
2 Do not use the printer near water.
3 Do not place the printer on an unstable table.
4 Transport it with care.
5 Cover it to protect it from dust.
6 Do not block or cover the slots provided for ventilation.
7 Check the plug to make sure it has been earthed.
8 Never use oil to lubricate moving parts.
9 Place the printer near the socket.
10 Do not attempt to service the printer yourself.

Die indirekte Rede im Aussagesatz und das Gesetz der Zeitenfolge

- Bei Aussagen *(statements)* verändert sich in der indirekten Rede nichts (außer der Verschiebung der Personen), wenn der einführende Satz im Präsens (selten im Perfekt oder im Futur) steht:

    Penny says, "I see the point."
    Penny says that she sees the point.

- Steht dagegen der einführende Satz *(She said that . . .)* in einer Zeit der Vergangenheit (Imperfekt oder Plusquamperfekt), so muß auch das Verb der indirekten Rede in einer Zeit der Vergangenheit stehen (Gesetz der Zeitenfolge). Dabei wird die Zeit des Verbs um eine Stufe weiter in die Vergangenheit gerückt.

    BEISPIELE
    Penny said, "I want a pay rise."
    Penny said that she wanted a pay rise.

    Penny said, "We replaced the old computer system."
    Penny said that they had replaced the old computer system.

    Penny said, "We will never use typewriters again."
    Penny said that they would never use typewriters again.

- Abweichungen vom Gesetz der Zeitenfolge

    ◇ Das Konditional (. . . würde . . .) kann nicht verschoben werden.
    Penny said, "I would go to the Furniture Fair."
    Penny said that she would go to the Furniture Fair.

    ◇ Das Plusquamperfekt kann nicht verschoben werden.
    Penny said, "I had finished my work."
    Penny said that she had finished her work.

    ◇ Das Präsens bleibt in der indirekten Rede erhalten, wenn ein objektiver Tatbestand, eine unumstößliche Wahrheit ausgedrückt wird.
    He said, "The sun is bigger than the moon."
    He said that the sun is bigger than the moon.

Übung 5

Lassen Sie Tom in indirekter Rede die einzelnen Sätze wiederholen, als ob er Kollegen erzählen wollte, was er gerade gehört hat.

BEISPIEL The electronics industry will create new jobs. (She said)
She said that the electronics industry would create new jobs.

1 The company has been in business for 15 years. (He said)
2 We planned to expand our range of products. (He added)
3 But some of our goods are difficult to store because of their short life-span. (He admitted)
4 Our stockholding costs have been too high. (They realized)
5 There hasn't been any demand for our products lately. (He added)
6 I had a good position here. (He said)
7 I have been made redundant. (He told me)
8 I will apply for a new job. (He said)
9 I am ready to take any risk. (He promised)
10 Are there any vacancies in your company? (He wanted to know)
11 Our advertising campaign was a great success. (She confirmed)
12 Yes, there was a problem. (She admitted)
13 All our sales literature got lost in the post. (She said)
14 We have always complied with the import regulations. (She assured us)
15 All the advertising material is always sent out on time. (She repeated)
16 All orders will be met on time (She was sure)
17 I want to change the supplier. (She explained)
18 They have given us very good discounts. (She added)
19 They always offer a wide range of choice. (She said)
20 The other firm has so far only sold its products in Asia. (She drew Tom's attention to the fact that)

Passiv und Verlaufsform in der indirekten Rede

♦ Das Passiv und die Verlaufsform, aber auch andere Konstruktionen wie z.B. to *be going to* folgen der einfachen Regel der Zeitenfolge, nämlich der Rücksetzung um eine Zeitstufe:

Penny said, "I am talking on the phone."
Penny said that she was talking on the phone.

Penny said, "I have been doing the accounts for ages."
Penny said that she had been doing the accounts for ages.

Tom said, "The letters are always opened immediately."
Tom said that the letters were always opened immediately.

Tom said, "The money was remitted on Tuesday."
Tom said that the money had been remitted on Tuesday.

Tom said, "The faulty goods will be replaced."
Tom said that the faulty goods would be replaced.

Übung 6

Setzen Sie die folgenden Sätze in die indirekte Rede, und finden Sie selbst Einleitungen in der Vergangenheit.

BEISPIEL   Some shops are hopelessly understaffed.
            She said that some shops were hopelessly understaffed.

1 Penny's replacement is going to type the letters.
2 I am going to meet Mr Grant right after the conference.
3 He will not be moved to another department.
4 He is having a word with the production manager.
5 I was checking the sales figures and she was working on the graphics.
6 The visitor has been waiting for half an hour.
7 The loss was offset immediately by a substantial price increase.
8 The conditions of the contract have been examined.
9 The invitations are just being typed.
10 She is going to take part in the induction scheme.
11 She is correcting her mistakes.
12 He has been working with Tinpot Construction for years.

Wortverschiebungen in der indirekten Rede

- Einige Wörter müssen bei der Umsetzung von der direkten in die indirekte Rede verschoben werden, weil es sonst zu Mißverständnissen kommen könnte. Wenden Sie die Verschiebungen zunächst mechanisch an; später werden Sie dann merken, daß nicht jedes *this* in *that* umgewandelt werden muß. Verschoben werden:

here	→ there
now	→ then, at once
today	→ that day
yesterday	→ the day before
tomorrow	→ the following day
last week	→ the week before, the previous week
next week	→ the following week
... ago	→ before
this, these	→ that, those
not (...) yet	→ until then

Übung 7

Wählen Sie eine der folgenden Einleitungen aus und setzen Sie die Sätze in die indirekte Rede: they said, we heard, she remarked, he stated, she explained, we added, they promised.

BEISPIEL   I have always worked here.
She said that she had always worked there.

1. We received your consignment yesterday.
2. I am positive that the meeting today will be a short one.
3. The company has always been based here.
4. I filed my tax return last week.
5. She applied for the job three weeks ago but did not turn up for the interview.
6. Last week the complaint was settled by arbitration.
7. We have finished the shortlist and are preparing the schedule for the interviews today.
8. We have not got any details now.

9   They are talking about a strike now but they have not considered the long-term effect.
10 I will not have the results till next week.
11 These items are very reasonably priced.
12 We will cancel our contract with them tomorrow if they do not give any reasons for the delay.
13 I won't reject this offer.
14 The invoice was settled about six weeks ago.
15 The consignment we received yesterday was three weeks late.
16 It means that we will have to do overtime next month.

Die Frage in der indirekten Rede

♦   Auf eine Frage in der indirekten Rede wird keine Antwort erwartet, sondern man gibt nur die Tatsache wieder, daß gefragt wurde. Deshalb entfällt auch die Umschreibung mit *to do*. Die Verschiebung der Zeiten findet wie im Aussagesatz statt.

   He asked, "Do you know?"
   He asked if (whether) I knew.

   I wanted to know, "Can he go?"
   I wanted to know if (whether) he could go.

♦   Der Anschluß der indirekten Frage erfolgt, wie man aus den obigen Beispielen sieht, mit *if* oder *whether*. Enthält die direkte Frage ein Fragewort (*where, when, what, who* usw.), so wird mit dem gleichen Fragewort angeschlossen.

   He asked, "What will she do?"
   He asked what she would do.

   She asked, "When do you expect me?"
   She asked when we expected her.

Übung 8

Stellen Sie die folgenden Fragen indirekt, indem Sie ask als einleitendes Verb benutzen. Beachten Sie, daß in einer indirekten Frage die Umschreibung mit to do entfällt.

BEISPIEL   Do you use French in your job?
She asked if (whether) I used French in my job.

1 Is recession a problem in your country?
2 Have you chosen an agent for the new market?
3 Do they have sufficient capital?
4 Does she already know how to fill in the form correctly?
5 Is he in charge of the laboratory?
6 Can we have a breakdown of costs?
7 May I use your telephone?
8 Does the time suit you?
9 Is the cheque negotiable?
10 Do they charge by volume or by weight?
11 Did you put in a claim for compensation?
12 Have you received the insurance certificate?
13 Can you calculate the premium for this consignment?
14 Will our account be overdrawn?
15 Have the expenses been refunded?

Übung 9

In diesen Sätzen gehen Sie vor wie in der vorhergehenden Übung, nur haben Sie hier zwischen Hauptsatz und Nebensatz ein Fragepronomen.

BEISPIELE   What are their difficulties?
He asked what their difficulties were.
How much did the meal with the sales people cost?
She asked how much the meal with the sales people had cost.

1 How can we cut down on travel costs?
2 What did he say during the meeting?
3 Where did you put last month's figures?
4 What do you think of our new SX models?

5 What skills are needed for this job?
6 What is the unemployment situation in your part of the country like?
7 How long have you been working for them?
8 How many workers do they employ?
9 Where does the company have its headquarters?
10 What did they offer during the negotiations?
11 When did they file for bankruptcy?
12 What percentage of the costs does advertising account for?
13 Where can we get the proposal forms?
14 How can I get in touch with him?
15 When did the difficulties start?
16 What is their complaint about?
17 What is your area code, please?
18 What number have you dialled?

Die Kurzantworten in der indirekten Rede

♦ Die Kurzantworten auf die direkte Frage werden durch Wiederholung des Hilfszeitwortes (*can, must, have* usw.) oder durch Formen von *to do* gebildet. Genau das gleiche geschieht in der indirekten Rede. Allerdings werden *yes* und *no* weggelassen und die Regel der Zeitenfolge muß beachtet werden.

direkt	indirekt
He asked, "Did you see me?" I replied, "No, I *didn't.*"	He asked whether I had seen him. I replied that I *hadn't*.
He asked, "Do you understand?" I replied, "Yes, I *do*."	He asked if I understood. I replied that I *did*.
We asked, "Can you deliver from stock?" They said, "Yes, we *can*."	We asked if they could deliver from stock. They said that they *could*.

Übung 10

Bilden Sie indirekte Fragen und Antworten. Die einleitenden Verben sind vorgegeben, und es ist angeführt, ob Sie eine positive oder negative Antwort geben sollen.

BEISPIEL   Do you have any dealings with Brown Ltd?
(They wanted to know / I said – negative)
They wanted to know if we had any dealings with Brown Ltd. I said that we hadn't.

1. Did you offer them a $2,000 credit?
   (They wanted to know / We told them – negative)
2. Will you come to an agreement with them?
   (They asked / We answered – positive)
3. Have the goods found a market?
   (They wanted to know / We told them – positive)
4. Is this an order for immediate delivery?
   (We asked / They confirmed – positive)
5. Have they submitted an offer?
   (He wanted to know / We told him – negative)
6. Are you satisfied with our rates of pay?
   (He asked us / We said – positive)
7. Will our sales figures in this area recover?
   (We asked ourselves / Mrs Jenkins assured us – positive)
8. Are you satisfied with the results?
   (They wanted to know / We wrote to them – positive)
9. Was there any complaint about the sample?
   (They wanted to know / We told them – positive)
10. Will there be a delay in delivery?
    (They asked / We told them – negative)
11. Had they made the necessary arrangements?
    (I asked / They confirmed – positive)
12. Can you hold the goods for ten days?
    (They asked us / We answered – positive)

Die Hilfsverben in der indirekten Rede:
can - may - must

- In der Regel gilt für die unvollständigen Hilfsverben die Verschiebung der Zeiten, wobei man die bekannten Umschreibungen in den entsprechenden Zeitformen gebraucht *(can = to be able to; may = to be allowed to; must = to have to).*

    "I could not find you."
    He said that he had not been able to find me.

    "I had to do it."
    She said that she had had to do it.

Übung 11

Finden Sie selbst Einleitungen und setzen Sie die folgenden Sätze in die indirekte Rede.

BEISPIEL   We must test the product and find out if the complaints are justified.
They said that they had to test the product and find out if the complaints were justified.

1. We cannot rent a stand at the fair.
2. We must charge higher prices.
3. They need me here, so I cannot help you at the stand.
4. She must leave if she wants to catch the train.
5. You may not take it home for the weekend.
6. We could reduce prices for some of our articles.
7. We must launch a big advertising campaign on TV.
8. It is an introductory price. We cannot tell you what the final price will be.
9. We must update our instruction booklets.
10. Our service electrician could not carry out the repair work.
11. We must find somebody who speaks fluent English and German.
12. I could not start investigations immediately.

Zusammenfassende Übungen

Übung 12

**Geben Sie diesen Text in der indirekten Rede wieder.
Der Anfang könnte so lauten:**
At a press conference journalists were told that ...

A deal has been struck between trade unions and the Post Office authorities that will allow postmen to wear shorts. Although there are some postmen who have been wearing them for years already, this is the first time that shorts have been accepted as part of the postmen's dresscode. Shorts will be allowed if the temperature goes above 78° F. However, the shorts that are permitted must be dark and of Bermuda-length rather than running-shorts. In this way it is guaranteed that the shorts will be in keeping with the rest of the uniform. A postman wearing lilac beach shorts will not be allowed to go out on his round.

Übung 13

Dies ist ein Text über frühe elektronische Textverarbeitung. Setzen Sie ihn in die indirekte Rede und gebrauchen Sie verschiedene einführende Verben (say, add, remark, inform, explain).

There are some computers which can only do word processing. There are two basic types. A stand-alone system is intended for one operator only and can process texts. A communicating and shared-logic system, however, keeps several operators at different keyboards busy. Each of them has access to a central hard-disk.
Wordprocessors can perform many different sorts of office work: files can be stored on floppy-disks or on a central hard-disk. Once a document has been keyed in and stored, it can be called up on the screen and worked on. Old information can be removed and new paragraphs can be added. The layout of a letter can be altered without difficulty. Any data stored or loaded into the computer's memory can be combined with an already existing text. The screen will show you exactly what the wordprocessor is going to print.

Übung 14

Die folgenden Sätze sind in die indirekte Rede zu setzen. Finden Sie eigene einleitende Verben.

BEISPIEL   We hope to make a good profit at the end of the year.
Mr Reade said that they hoped to make good profit at the end of the year.

1   The trial order was completed to our full satisfaction.
2   They have to invest quite a lot of money in their factory extension.
3   Penny was not wrong to give such a frank opinion.
4   Train connections to Mid-Wales are very bad.
5   They have been in business for more than six years.
6   They are going to launch their new line in October.
7   We will have to cut back on expenditure.
8   Even our competitors say that our new line is very attractive.
9   I expect to come to an agreement with Bryant Systems soon.
10 We will have to overcome the financial difficulties.
11 Our agent is most certainly not going to offer a bigger reduction.
12 He does not think it is a bargain.
13 The decisions we have to make require skill and judgement.
14 It took me six months to find a new job.
15 Three years ago Susan worked in the personnel department.
16 At breakeven point you neither earn a profit nor suffer a loss.
17 Tom, you must provide a monthly, not a weekly report.
18 We must try some minor alterations.

Das Passiv

Einführung

- Die Form des Passivs ist im Englischen besonders wichtig, da sie viel häufiger verwendet wird als im Deutschen. Im Gespräch und in der Korrespondenz stellt sie die Sache in den Vordergrund, während die Person zurücktritt.
  Aktiv: *Your employees apparently damaged two cases before shipment.*
  Passiv: *Two cases were apparently damaged before shipment.*

- Bei der Bildung des Passivs wird das Objekt des Aktivsatzes zum Subjekt des Passivsatzes. (Das alte Subjekt kann im Passiv mit *by* hinten angefügt werden.)

	Subjekt	Prädikat	
Aktiv	*Penny*	*wrote*	*the letter.*
Passiv	*The letter*	*was written*	*by Penny.*

- Das Passiv wird aus einer Form von *to be* und dem Partizip Perfekt gebildet. Bei unregelmäßigen Verben ist das die dritte Form (to write, wrote, *written*), bei regelmäßigen Verben wird die Form durch Anhängen der Endung -*ed* gebildet (z.B. *opened*)

Präsens	*am, are, is*	*The letter is written.* wird geschrieben
Imperfekt	*was, were*	*The letter was written.* wurde geschrieben
Perfekt	*has been,* *have been*	*The letter has been written.* ist geschrieben worden

Plusquamperfekt	had been	The letter had been written. war geschrieben worden
Futur 1	shall be, will be	The letter will be written. wird geschrieben werden
Futur 2	shall/will have been	The letter will have been written. wird geschrieben worden sein
Konditional 1	should be, would be	The letter would be written würde geschrieben werden
Konditional 2	should/would have been	The letter would have been written wäre geschrieben worden
Verlaufsform Präsens	am/are/is being	The letter is being written.
Verlaufsform Imperfekt	was/were being	The letter was being written.

Übung 1

Setzen Sie die folgenden Passivsätze nacheinander in die beiden in den Klammern angegebenen Zeiten.

BEISPIEL The documents are prepared. (Perf., Fut. 1)
The documents have been prepared.
The documents will be prepared.

1 The invoice was settled. (Fut. 1, Perf.)
2 The contract is cancelled. (Kond. 1, Kond. 2)
3 Their offer will be rejected. (Präs., Imp.)
4 Our new canteen has been finished. (Fut. 1, Plusqu.)
5 The agenda of the meeting was discussed. (Plusqu., Kond. 2)
6 The new system has been installed. (Fut. 1, Imp.)
7 This problem is not solved. (Perf., Kond. 1)

Das alte Subjekt des Aktivsatzes

- Das alte Subjekt des Aktivsatzes kann dann mit *by* hinten angefügt werden, wenn es für die Aussage wichtig ist. Es soll z.B. betont werden, wer die Anweisungen gegeben hat oder was einen Vorgang ausgelöst hat.

  The instructions were given by Mrs Jenkins.

- Die Ergänzung entfällt, wenn es sich um *you, someone, people, they* und ähnliche unbestimmte Personenangaben handelt.

  Someone has removed the packaging.
  The packaging has been removed.

Übung 2

Setzen Sie die folgenden Sätze ins Passiv und bei Sätzen 16-20 entscheiden Sie, ob der Handelnde mit by angeschlossen wird.

BEISPIEL   The board of directors discussed the problem. (agent)
The problem was discussed by the board of directors.

1. We all keep our line managers informed. (no agent)
2. They suggested several changes. (no agent)
3. Computers have improved distribution considerably. (agent)
4. Have they packed the goods? (no agent)
5. Workers have put these cases on the lorries. (no agent)
6. He buys goods in great quantities. (no agent)
7. He holds the goods until the retailer asks for them. (no agent, two passives)
8. In this way the wholesaler keeps up a steady flow of production. (no agent)
9. The manufacturer recalled all the faulty cars. (no agent)
10. That is why they need predictions about the market. (no agent)
11. First they produced components, then they manufactured machines, now they offer complete systems. (no agent, three passives)
12. They will trade raw materials for high quality western products. (no agent)

13 They interpreted the agreement in a different way. (no agent)
14 They will put that point on the agenda. (no agent)
15 This product will probably trigger a furious reaction. (agent)
16 He submitted his report to the board two weeks ago.
17 Our company won a substantial contract for office furniture.
18 The committee has discussed the ideas.
19 The Board of Directors will elect the chairperson.
20 We will send the goods to you on Friday.

Übung 3

In diesem Text geht es um die Rolle des Großhändlers, der zwischen Herstellung und Einzelhandel vermittelt.
Übertragen Sie die Sätze bzw. Satzteile ins Passiv. Die <u>unterstrichenen</u> Wörter bilden das neue Subjekt.

Wholesalers

The wholesaler buys goods[1] in bulk from the manufacturer. He keeps them[2] in stock until the retailer requires them[3]. Of course he charges a fee[4] for this service, i.e. he raises the selling price[5].

People often consider the wholesaler's part[6] unnecessary. In fact, however, the wholesaler helps both the manufacturer and the retailer[7]. Wholesalers have always controlled the flow of goods between manufacturers and retailers[8]. The wholesaler reduces the manufacturer's costs[9] as he reduces the need to store finished products in warehouses. Retailers like this arrangement because they can buy goods[10] in smaller quantities.

In many cases wholesalers offer credit[11] to the retailers so that they do not have to look for loans anywhere else. But the modern economy has weakened the wholesaler's position[12]. New methods of distribution have reduced his or her importance[13]. Many manufacturers have eliminated the wholesaler[14] completely through direct selling. Some of the wholesaler's former customers buy in bulk themselves.

Das Passiv bei Verben mit Präpositionen

- Verben, die mit einer bestimmten Präposition verwendet werden, müssen diese Präposition auch im Passivsatz beibehalten.

They talked about the terms of payment.
The terms of payment were talked about.

Übung 4

Setzen Sie die folgenden Sätze ins Passiv und lassen Sie die Ergänzung mit by weg, wenn Sie sie für entbehrlich halten.

BEISPIEL   Why have they put off the interview?
Why has the interview been put off?

1   The staff approved of his appointment.
2   When should I pick him up from his hotel?
3   Who did we hire the lorry from?
4   Why have you not taken out an insurance policy?
5   People took a lot of notice of this new material.
6   Who did they recommend him to?
7   They pay a lot of attention to sales exhibitions.
8   Has anybody brought up the question of the new markets in Eastern Europe?
9   They all make use of the new photocopier.
10   Everybody laughed at the misprints in our new catalogue.
11   We took account of her youth in her appraisal.
12   Who did they address the letter to?
13   What have they congratulated Penny on?
14   All I can see is his incompetence and that is not what we pay him for.
15   Will they look after the trainees properly?

Das Passiv mit Hilfsverben

- Viele Hilfsverben bilden ihre Ersatzformen schon im Passiv (wie *to be obliged to, to be forced to, to be allowed to*). An Hilfsverben, die nicht in einer Form des Passives auftreten, hängt man *be* und das Partizip Perfekt (wie bei *can, could, may, must, shall, should, have to* und *ought to*).

The goods can be delivered from stock.
Office paper must be used .
It might be done by the office junior.
The boxes ought to be checked on arrival.
It should be reported to the production manager.

Übung 5

In den folgenden Sätzen, in denen es um die Besetzung einer freien Stelle geht, finden Sie Hilfsverben. Übertragen Sie die Sätze ins Passiv.

BEISPIEL   Candidates have to pass a psychological test.
A psychological test has to be passed.

1. We had to place an advertisement in the local paper.
2. Our personnel manager thought that we could not consider in-company recruitment.
3. Miss Powell had to provide a detailed job description.
4. You could use our company's general application form.
5. We had to write a reference for one of our employees.
6. Ruth, our assistant personnel manager, ought to check all the references.
7. We can short-list four candidates.
8. We must arrange appointments for the interviews.
9. Mr Reade may select four members for the interview panel.
10. Our personnel department has to prepare a contract of employment.

Übung 6

Im folgenden geht es um die Ausführung eines Auftrags. Setzen Sie die Sätze ins Passiv. Achten Sie auf die richtige Zeit.

BEISPIEL   What price does the supplier charge for this kind of product?
What price is charged for this kind of product?

Letter of Inquiry
1 Can the supplier fix a delivery date?
2 Does he offer credit?
3 A customer will write more than one letter of inquiry.
4 Thus he can compare goods and prices.

Quotation
5 The potential supplier will send a quotation.
6 The potential customer might find the terms of trade in a price-list.
7 The unit price is the recommended retail price, i.e. the price which the consumer has to pay. (The unit price is ...)
8 The supplier will offer a trade discount.
9 It is a reduction that the manufacturer grants.
10 In this way the retailer can make a profit.
11 If the retailer buys great quantities, the supplier might grant bulk or quantity discounts. (If the retailer ...)

Terms of Delivery
12 *carriage paid*
    The supplier will pay for the cost of transportation.
13 *carriage forward*
    The customer has to pay a fee for delivery.
14 *ex works*
    The manufacturer charges the buyer with all the costs after the goods leave the factory or the warehouse.
15 *F O R (free on rail)*
    The quoted price includes the cost of delivery to the railway terminal nearest the seller.
16 *F A S (free alongside ship)*
    The seller states a price that includes delivery to the dockside. The buyer takes care of freight, insurance and loading charges. (A price ...)

17 *F O B (free on board)*
   The seller pays the charge for the loading as well.
18 *C & F (cost and freight)*
   The seller's price includes delivery to the dockside and loading and freight charges to the customer's port.
19 *C I F (cost, insurance and freight)*
   The seller also pays the costs for the insurance to the port of destination.
20 *Landed*
   The exporter's price also includes the unloading charges at the port of destination.
21 *Franco*
   The seller (manufacturer) pays all the charges and delivers direct to his customer's premises. (All the charges … and he delivers …)

Terms of Payment
   Payment in advance
22 Usually the seller sends an invoice in advance of delivery.
23 He will only ship the goods when the invoice is settled.
   C O D (cash on delivery)
24 The buyer must pay the carrier in cash.
25 Both parties can agree upon special credit terms.
26 The seller will always encourage the buyer to pay promptly.
27 Sellers have always offered cash discounts for early payment.
28 Thus they avoid the trouble of sending reminders.

Übung 7

Versuchen Sie, die folgenden Beschwerden durch die Verwendung des Passivs etwas höflicher zu formulieren.

BEISPIEL   You have put us in a very awkward position.
            We have been put in a very awkward position.

1 You have made this mistake twice.
2 You misunderstood the terms of payment.
3 You should have examined the goods on arrival.
4 Apparently you have not read our operating instructions.

5 You made a mistake when you prepared the consignment for despatch. (two passives)
6 You must collect the cupboards we did not order.
7 I will cancel the whole order if you do not deliver by the end of the week. (two passives)
8 We will place our order elsewhere if you inform us you cannot complete it on time. (three passives)
9 We realize that you made quite a number of mistakes.
10 You have charged the unbelievable sum of $3000 for equipment I did not order. (two passives)
11 You must solve the problem without delay.
12 You should give us an explanation.
13 You must look into the matter asap (as soon as possible).
14 You should have sent the letter much earlier.

Übung 8

Setzen Sie die Sätze ins Passiv.

1 We must reach the breakeven point by November this year.
2 They have equipped our department with the most modern office machinery.
3 Where should we base the new department?
4 This new machine would tie up all our capital.
5 They have not yet paid our last invoice.
6 We will draw up a shortlist of candidates that are suitable for the position.
7 So far we have interviewed only one third of the applicants.
8 They will have to weigh up the two alternatives.
9 We will exchange the faulty CD players for new ones.
10 We had to replace the damaged parts immediately.
11 I will only accept conditions that compare favourably with those of our competitors.
12 Our agent must represent our interests there.
13 They would cover the loss.
14 A chairperson controls a meeting.
15 You will have to follow our operating instructions closely.
16 They never mentioned his name again.

Das Passiv bei Sätzen mit zwei Objekten

♦ Es gibt viele Verben, die zwei Objekte nach sich haben, meist ein persönliches (unterstrichen) und ein sachliches (*kursiv*) Objekt.

They offered us *new terms of payment*.
They offered *new terms of payment* to us.

♦ Bei der Passivbildung wählen Sie einfach das erste der beiden Objekte, meistens ist es das persönliche, und machen es zum Subjekt Ihres Passivsatzes.

We were offered *new terms of payment*.
New terms of payment were offered to us.

Übung 9

Setzen Sie die folgenden Sätze ins Passiv und verwenden Sie dabei ein persönliches Subjekt.

BEISPIEL   He granted them a pay rise.
They were granted a pay rise.

1 They denied non-members the right to take part in the meeting.
2 They have made Bill Mitchell shop steward.
3 Her line manager offered her a room on the second floor.
4 A junior clerk gave the new shop steward the key to his office.
5 Somebody handed Bill a box full of letters of complaint.
6 One of the cleaners complained that they had not granted her sick pay.
7 An employee wrote that they had refused her a day off for her sister's wedding.
8 They did not show Sarah the confidential report.
9 Harry was annoyed because they had offered his younger colleague higher wages.
10 Obviously they had not shown the secretary her job appraisal.
11 A group of workers stated that management had promised them better lighting, but nothing had been done so far.
12 The managing director offered Bill a more senior position in the company.

Das Passiv in der Verlaufsform

- Die Verlaufsform wird verwendet, wenn ein Vorgang gerade stattfindet. Das geht im Passiv nur in zwei Zeiten: dem Präsens und dem Imperfekt.
  - Wenn es sich um zwei gleichzeitig verlaufende Vorgänge handelt, wird *while* verwendet.
    The machine is being serviced while the workers are cleaning the floor.
  - Wenn es um einen Vorgang geht, der noch andauert, während ein anderer beginnt, wird *when* verwendet.
    The goods were being packed when we entered.

Übung 10

Setzen Sie den ersten Satz ins Passiv und verbinden Sie die beiden Sätze mit when oder mit while.

BEISPIELE They were considering wages and salaries. – News of industrial action was pouring in.
Wages and salaries were being considered while news of industrial action was pouring in.
We were preparing legal action. – We heard that they were willing to accept our proposal.
Legal action was being prepared when we heard that they were willing to accept our proposal.

1 We were just launching our new product. – The strike began.
2 They were cleaning the assembly line. – The operators were checking the new programme.
3 We were typing the delivery note. – They cancelled the order.
4 The insurance agent was examining the rest of the burnt cases. – Mr Reade was putting some questions to the foreman.
5 They were training her for the position of personal assistant. – They were installing a new communication system.
6 They were offering the paintbrushes at reduced prices. – They learned that the costs of raw materials had been increased.

7 We were cleaning the typewriter. – The mechanic arrived.
8 Our drivers were delivering the goods they had ordered the week before. – We heard that the company had been wound up.
9 She was informing the secretaries. – The telephone rang.
10 We were just setting up our new branch in Togo. – The Ministry of Trade abolished foreign exchange controls.
11 They were setting up a new production line. – They heard that their competitor was on the point of introducing an attractive new model, too.
12 They were retraining him for another job. – He was still drawing unemployment benefit.
13 They were preparing the stock room for the goods. – He found that the order had not been confirmed.
14 He is checking the quotation. – Susan is looking for last year's price list.

Das deutsche ‚man'

◆ Das deutsche ‚man' wird im Englischen am besten durch Passiv-Konstruktionen ausgedrückt.

You can find computer shops everywhere nowadays.
Computer shops can be found everywhere nowadays.
Computergeschäfte kann man heutzutage überall finden.

◆ Man kann einen Satz auch mit einer persönlichen Wendung einleiten. Diese Form ist im Englischen überaus gebräuchlich.

They are expected to make a counteroffer.
Man erwartet von ihnen ein Gegenangebot.

She is said to be the best salesperson the company has ever had.
Man sagt von ihr, sie sei die beste Verkäuferin, die die Firma je gehabt hat.

- Man kann einen Satz passivisch mit einer unpersönlichen Wendung einleiten, wie *it is said* (man sagt), *it is believed* (man glaubt), *it is supposed* (man nimmt an), *it is expected* (man erwartet) usw.

It is expected that they will make a counteroffer.
Man erwartet, daß sie ein Gegenangebot machen werden.

It is said that she is the best salesperson the company has ever had.
Man sagt, daß sie die beste Verkäuferin ist, die die Firma je gehabt hat.

Übung 11

Setzen Sie folgende Sätze ins Passiv und leiten Sie die Sätze jeweils mit einer unpersönlichen Wendung ein, wie it is said, it is believed / assumed / supposed usw.

BEISPIEL They say that he has been in prison.
It is said that he has been in prison.

1 We suppose that they will change their selling policy.
2 They all assume that we are doing a brisk trade in kitchen stools. (It is generally . . .)
3 They say that he was expelled from school because of indiscipline.
4 We assume that their losses due to the flood were immense.
5 We fear that our journal has suffered quite a loss in advertising revenue.
6 They say they have got enough money to finish their new office building.
7 They believe that computers take people's jobs away.
8 People say that the profits from their exports are eaten up by the losses in the domestic market.
9 People say that he is an excellent salesman.
10 People believe that their campaign was a complete flop.

Übung 12

Setzen Sie folgende Sätze ins Passiv und leiten Sie die Sätze jeweils mit einer persönlichen Wendung ein.

BEISPIEL   It is said that Bill is a tough negotiator.
Bill is said to be a tough negotiator.

1 It is said that she is the brains within the company.
2 It is assumed that she has applied for the vacant position of head of sales promotion.
3 It is said that he is a billionaire.
4 It is believed that thousands of investors have lost everything with Lloyds.
5 It is known that they carry out opinion surveys.
6 It is said that he is one of the high fliers in the company.
7 It is supposed that his job is safe.
8 It is expected that we will have more redundancies.
9 It is said that she keeps strictly confidential papers in her drawer.
10 It is known that they pay promptly.

Übung 13

Setzen Sie in dieser gemischten Übung folgende Sätze ins Passiv.

1 I have called this meeting to look into ways of raising more capital.
2 They paid a lot of attention to the sales figures.
3 We are going to check the list.
4 Tom treated Penny to a snack.
5 They offered us payment by irrevocable letter of credit.
6 Why did he mention it again?
7 After that very poor year, we had expected a change in leadership.
8 We had compared prices carefully before we placed the order. (two passives)
9 They have secured several substantial orders from the Continent.
10 Somebody must have connected the fax machine incorrectly.
11 We expect that the secretary will find the mislaid contract. (two possible answers)
12 We can give him an office on the second floor.

13 The chairperson explained the problem to us.
14 We paid a lot of attention to their warning.
15 They assume that productivity can be increased.
16 We can cancel our contract with them at six months' notice.
17 They had ordered the goods from their old supplier.
18 They say that delegating is an important management skill.
19 We promised our new customers express delivery. (two possible answers)
20 You have made a mistake in your addition.
21 We must avoid a breakdown in communication.
22 These people are analyzing the organization.
23 We did not take any notice of the memo. (two possible answers)
24 They believe that more workers will be made redundant.
25 In this way we will reduce our marketing costs.
26 They are just announcing the annual results.

Übung 14

Übertragen Sie die Sätze vom Passiv zurück ins Aktiv. Sie müssen das Subjekt des Aktivsatzes öfter selbst finden.

BEISPIEL   He was seen when he climbed out of the window.
They saw him when he climbed out of the window.

1 These new agents are not fully trained.
2 Their proposal was not accepted.
3 We have always been given good service.
4 He will be transferred abroad next year.
5 The target date for the shipment will be met.
6 I think he can be persuaded to give in.
7 All this must be done before shipment.
8 The prices must be renegotiated.
9 Because of the strike no more than 30% of the order could be supplied.
10 Contract negotiations will be left to Mrs Jenkins.
11 The annual accounts are being prepared right now.
12 If you plan carefully in advance, transit time can be reduced.
13 The goods will be transferred from one vehicle to another.
14 The goods will have to be placed in a bonded warehouse.

Die Zeiten 4

Einführung

- Da das englische System der Zeiten vom deutschen nur in Einzelfällen abweicht, gibt es vom Verständnis der Grammatik her auch nur wenig Schwierigkeiten. Eigentlich braucht man z.b. die Begriffe Bedingungsform (Konditional) und vollendete Vergangenheit (Plusquamperfekt) gar nicht zu erklären, sie laufen dem deutsen Sprachgebrauch parallel.

- Es gibt zwei grammatische Zeiten *(tenses)* im Englischen, die sich vom Deutschen unterscheiden.

  - **Die Verlaufsform** (*progressive* oder *continuous form*), die ausdrückt, daß etwas zu einer bestimmten Zeit gerade geschieht, und die es deshalb theoretisch in allen grammatischen Zeiten gibt. Diese Form existiert im Deutschen nicht.

  - **Das Perfekt** (*present perfect*)
    Diese Zeit wird abweichend vom Deutschen im Englischen nach festen Regeln angewendet.

Die Verlaufsform

- Die Verlaufsform wird aus einer Form von *to be* und dem Partizip Präsens gebildet (das ist die *ing*-Form eines Verbs, z.B. *raining*).

Präsens	am, are, is	She is typing the letter. tippt gerade
Imperfekt	was, were	She was typing the letter. tippte gerade

Perfekt	has been, have been	She has been typing the letter. hat gerade getippt
Plusquamperfekt	had been	She had been typing the letter. hatte gerade getippt
Futur	(shall be), will be	She will be typing the letter. wird gerade tippen
Konditional	(should be), would be	She would be typing the letter. würde gerade tippen

- Die Verlaufsform drückt aus, daß in einer bestimmten Zeit gerade etwas geschieht. Oft signalisieren Adverbien (*now, at the moment*, etc), daß der Vorgang gerade abläuft.

- Meistens handelt es sich um einen Vorgang, der vorübergehend andauert und noch nicht abgeschlossen ist.

Übung 1

Bilden Sie anhand der Signalwörter oder des Kontexts die Verlaufsform. Es handelt sich um a junior clerk's duties.

BEISPIEL From time to time he makes a cup of tea for a visitor.
(At the moment . . .)
At the moment he is making a cup of tea for a visitor.

1 Every morning Tom opens the letters.
 (Look, . . .)
2 He distributes letters to the in-trays for the appropriate departments.
 (Now . . .)
3 He empties the out-trays in various departments.
 (At the moment . . .)
4 Sometimes he helps the filing clerks in the filing room.
 (Now . . .)
5 Sometimes he looks for a document wanted by the filing clerk.
 (He is worried; he . . .)

6 He collects all outgoing mail from the clerks.
   (... just ...)
7 Between 3.30 and 4.00 p.m. he puts all the out-going mail in envelopes.
   (Look at Tom, ...)
8 Then he seals the envelopes.
   (What is he doing now? He ...)
9 Before the office closes Tom goes from door to door distributing the interdepartmental mail.
   (Can you see him? He ...)
10 Before he goes home he helps out in the company's post room.
   (Now ...)

Übung 2

Susan ist die Sekretärin von Mrs Jenkins, der vielbeschäftigten Verkaufsleiterin der Firma. Vervollständigen Sie die Sätze und sagen Sie, was Susan gerade tut.

BEISPIEL   At nine she comes to the office and makes a cup of tea.
           It is nine o'clock. Susan ...
           Susan is making a cup of tea.

1 At 9.30 she prepares the morning's correspondence for Mrs Jenkins.
   It is 9.30. She ...
2 At ten she takes some urgent letters to Mrs Jenkins' office.
   It is ten o'clock. She ...
3 At l0.30 she rings several customers for Mrs Jenkins.
   It is 10.30.
4 At eleven they both have a cup of tea.
   It is eleven.
5 At 11.15 Mrs Jenkins talks to her about preparing some new contracts.
   It is 11.15.
6 From eleven to one o'clock Susan keys the contracts into the computer.
   It is a quarter past eleven.
7 At one o'clock Susan goes to the canteen with her colleagues.
   It is one o'clock.
8 At 2.00 p.m. she receives visitors who have an appointment.
   It is 2.00 p.m.

Das einfache Präsens

- Das einfache Präsens *(simple present)* drückt aus:
  - einen Zustand von Dauer
    Ian works for Brown Ltd.
  - etwas, das immer so ist
    Everybody respects the chairperson.
  - etwas, das regelmäßig geschieht oder gewohnheitsmäßig getan wird
    A secretary prepares the agenda.
    The supervisor never goes home before 6 p.m.
  - etwas, das berufsmäßig getan wird
    The accountant keeps the accounts.

Übung 3

Vervollständigen Sie die Sätze und verwenden Sie entweder das einfache Präsens (simple present) oder die Verlaufsform.

BEISPIELE Every morning he (dictate) letters at ten.
Every morning he dictates letters at ten.
Where is Tom? He (take part) in a training course for junior clerks.
He is taking part in a training course for junior clerks.

1 Our company (employ) 140 people.
2 Susan is busy. She (work) on the route for Mrs Jenkins' trip to North Africa.
3 All the newspapers are full of the SX 400. Wilsher & Co. (advertise) their new model wherever they can.
4 They (interview) every applicant. That's company policy. (zwei Formen möglich)
5 You should know how to operate it. Watch, first you (switch) it on here.
6 Don't disturb him. He (have) a word with Tom.
7 This is our marketing strategy: we (offer) a free manual with every machine we sell.

8 You can have last year's model cheaper since we (have) a stock clearance.
9 The meeting is on and Mr Reade (chair) it.
10 Our packaging (provide) adequate protection for the goods.
11 I have tried everything to contact him. Which hotel he (stay) at?
12 I cannot find the draft of the contract, so I (retype) it.
13 You will not find him in his office. He (show) visitors round the factory.
14 Why he (want) to leave the company?
15 Good morning, Mr Collier. Mrs Jenkins (expect) you.
16 Tell me how many pencils one box (contain).

Übung 4

Sie finden hier Auszüge aus Gesprächen. Ersetzen Sie die in Klammern angegebenen Infinitiv-Formen durch das einfache Präsens oder die Verlaufsform.

1 A   What (do) top executives?
  B   They (plan) and (carry out) company policy.
2 A   What is the job of someone who (belong) to the middle management of a company?
  B   They (make) the day-to-day decisions.
3 A   And what is a supervisor paid for?
  B   He or she (look after) the delivery of the supplies, (sort out) any technical problems, and (check) whether the work is being done properly.
4 A   I see, but look at Mr Williams over there. He just (stare) at us; he (not do) anything.
  B   Perhaps he (check up) on you.
5 A   I am new here. I can see so many people in this office who (work) hard. Who's that lady over there?
  B   Mrs Turner. She (talk) to another new employee.
6 A   Who is the man who (wear) a short sleeved shirt and (stand) in the corner over there?
  B   That's Bill, our shop steward.
  A   What he (do) in the secretary's office?
  B   I (not know) exactly. His job is to represent the employees and workers. Maybe he (listen) to a complaint.

7 B The young man on your right is Tom. Look, he (go) from office to office and (collect) today's letters for signatures.
  A And what (happen) to them when they are signed?
  B Tom (take) them to the company's post room and he (hand) the copies to the filing clerk.
8 The young lady here is Penny. She is a clerical assistant. She (do) all sorts of clerical work.
  B Hello, Penny, meet Sam Brown, our new control clerk. Can you tell him what you (usually do)?
  P I usually (work) in the filing department, but at the moment I (type) letters for the sales department. Susan, Mrs Jenkins' secretary, is on holiday.
9 A Who is the lady in the navy blue blouse? She just (cross) the room.
  B She is the sales manager, Mrs Jenkins. She (have) a difficult time at the moment because she has been without her secretary for two weeks.
10 During lunch break, Sam Brown (meet) Penny in the canteen.
  A Hello, remember me? I'm Sam Brown, the new control clerk. (wait) you for me?
  P No, actually, I (wait) for Tom, – we always (have) lunch together. But do please sit down and join us.

Übung 5

Ordnen Sie die Satzhälften einander zu.

BEISPIEL   1 He checks the sales figures
           2 He is checking the sales figures
              a so don't disturb him.
              b every Monday morning.
           Lösung: *1b, 2a*

3 We are sending it under separate cover
4 We send it under separate cover
   a if it weighs more than two kilos.
   b as it comes from a different department.

5 They service the photocopier
6 They are servicing the photocopier
   a   so you cannot do any copying now.
   b   once a year.
7 Tom helps Penny
8 Tom is helping Penny
   a   whenever he has time.
   b   as it is 5.30 already.
9 Susan leaves Mrs Jenkins a message
10 Susan is leaving Mrs Jenkins a message
   a   because she has to go home early today.
   b   before she goes home if there is an urgent problem.
11 What sort of accommodation do you look for
12 What sort of accommodation are you looking for
   a   on a business trip?
   b   this time?
13 Our sprayguns are selling well
14 Our sprayguns sell well
   a   at the beginning of spring.
   b   because now is the time of year when people tend to decorate.
15 We are discussing various questions
16 We discuss various questions
   a   at every board meeting.
   b   so we can adapt ourselves to the changing economic situation.
17 He is drafting the letter himself
18 He drafts the letter himself
   a   and needs some additional information.
   b   if it is an important customer.
19 He is instructing the salesmen
20 He instructs the salesmen
   a   as the new model will be launched this week.
   b   at least once a week.
21 We are doing our best to get it ready on time
22 We do our best to get it ready on time
   a   if there is a penalty clause.
   b   as the express van is waiting in the yard.

Verben, die keine Verlaufsform bilden

- Wenn Verben keinen Vorgang, keine Handlung oder Tätigkeit beschreiben, können sie nicht in der Verlaufsform gebraucht werden. Dabei handelt es sich um Verben, die folgendes ausdrücken:

  ◊ einen Zustand
  to be, to have, to own, to possess, to belong to, to contain, to become, to seem, to look (aussehen), *to stay* (bleiben) usw.

  ◊ ein Gefühl oder ein Bedürfnis
  to (dis)like, to hate, to love, to mind, to prefer, to want, to need usw.

  ◊ das Ergebnis einer geistigen Tätigkeit
  to believe, to think, to mean, to know, to (dis)agree, to doubt usw.

  ◊ eine sinnliche Wahrnehmung
  to see, to hear, to smell, to taste, to feel

  ◊ Es gibt mehrere Verben, die zweierlei bedeuten.
  The soup tastes good. Mary likes it.
  The cook is tasting the soup right now.
  Die Suppe, die Mary schmeckt, tut nichts (*taste* bildet also keine Verlaufsform). Der Koch allerdings, der die Suppe abschmeckt, tut etwas (*taste* bildet also hier eine Verlaufsform).

Übung 6

Setzen Sie die Verben ins einfache Präsens oder in die Verlaufsform.

1 I am typing the letter now. Mrs Jenkins ... (want) me to.
2 Every meeting ... (need) a chairperson.
3 We have heard your proposals and we fully ... (agree).
4 The pen she is looking for is not hers, it ... (belong) to the supervisor.
5 We ... (hope) to find a new market for these luxury products. (zwei Formen möglich)
6 It is very annoying. They always ... (smoke) when there is a serious decision to be made.

7 He forgot his umbrella. Where is he now? He ... (sign) the visitors' book.
8 She ... (listen) to the workers' complaints and ... (agree) that conditions have to be improved.
9 It's a pity. Now we ... (regret) giving them the details.
10 I'm very optimistic. I ... (think) I can correct the mistake.
11 We ... (have) a lot of trouble with the new software at the moment.
12 Each of our secretaries ... (have) one of the new computers.
13 I'm afraid you have dialled the wrong number. We ... (not deal) in garden tools.
14 We ... (have) a new printer but nobody ... (know) how to operate it.
15 Yes, put him through, but first tell me what he ... (ring) about.
16 Hurry up. The flight ... (board) right now.
17 You said you had an idea about how we could improve office communication. What ... (have/you) in mind?
18 They ... (renew) their insurance every year.
19 Supervisors regularly ... (inspect) the quality of the glasses.
20 I ... (not like) the idea and I ... (doubt) whether we will penetrate the market with this new product.

Die Verlaufsform im Satzgefüge

- Die Verlaufsform steht auch, und zwar meistens im Imperfekt,

    - wenn zwei Vorgänge gleichzeitig stattfinden:
    While Tom was sealing the envelopes, Penny was operating the franking machine.

    - wenn eine Handlung einsetzt, während eine andere noch andauert:
    Mr Reade was dictating letters when Mrs Jenkins knocked at the door.

Übung 7

Vervollständigen Sie diese Sätze im Imperfekt gemäß der Beispiele.

BEISPIELE While they ... (assemble) the new range of machines, some of our workforce ... (produce) spare parts.
While they were assembling the new range of machines, some of our workforce were producing spare parts.
Penny ... (prepare) the report when the telephone rang.
Penny was preparing the report when the telephone rang.

1. Where ... (sit/you) when he came in? I ... (stand) by the window.
2. While Mrs Jenkins ... (travel) abroad, our marketing experts ... (prepare) the home market for our new powder coating system.
3. He ... (sit) at his desk drafting a letter to the insurance company when his line manager walked in.
4. What ... (do/they) when we arrived? They ... (look) for the video recorder for Mrs Jenkins' lecture on sales tactics.
5. Who did you have in mind as a replacement when you heard that he wanted to leave?
I ... (plan) to split the responsibilities and take on two stock-control clerks.
6. What ... (wait/you) for when the alarm bell rang?
7. The assistant ... (prepare) the shortlist while the personnel manager ... (interview) the first applicants.
8. She ... (access) a personal file on her computer when there was a sudden power-cut.
9. He ... (wait) for the managing director when the receptionist asked him about his flight.
10. While he ... (discuss) the terms of the agreement on the phone, he ... (note down) details for the next meeting.
11. What ... (do/you) when he suggested a merger? I ... (play) golf.
12. Why ... (drink/they) champagne when we saw them? They ... (celebrate) Bill's birthday.
13. What ... (do/you) when you heard about the accident? We ... (celebrate) my secretary's birthday.
14. They ... (work) on the new distribution system when their sales suddenly dropped.
15. What ... (discuss/they) when they heard about the strike?

Übung 8

Ordnen Sie die Satzhälften einander zu.

1 They were discussing how the training could be improved
2 They discussed how the training could be improved
    a   to meet the needs of new staff.
    b   when the managing director walked in.
3 He was removing the protective guard from the paper-trimmer
4 He removed the protective guard from the paper trimmer
    a   and fixed a new blade.
    b   when he cut his finger.
5 We were opening the shredder
6 We opened the shredder
    a   to remove the paper that had blocked the machine.
    b   when the safety officer entered the office.
7 He inspected the raw materials
8 He was inspecting the raw materials
    a   and then called the chief buyer.
    b   when the first complaints from the production department came in.
9 He was carefully reading the instructions
10 He carefully read the instructions
    a   and then assembled the machine.
    b   when Tom suddenly rushed in without knocking.
11 They were practising emergency procedures
12 They practised emergency procedures
    a   when they noticed the smoke coming out of the stockroom.
    b   twice a year in accordance with the "Health and Safety at Work Act".

Die Verlaufsform im Passiv

- Die Verlaufsform gibt es auch im Passiv, aber sie wird nur in wenigen Zeiten eingesetzt.
  Wir können uns auf zwei Zeitstufen beschränken:

  ◊ **Präsens**
  They are just being inspected.
  Sie werden gerade geprüft.

  ◊ **Imperfekt**
  They were being inspected.
  Sie wurden gerade geprüft.

Übung 9

Setzen Sie die Verben in die richtige Form der Verlaufsform Passiv.

BEISPIELE   What are their conditions? I don't know yet, they ... just ... (be examined).
They are just being examined.
What did you tell him when he rang up? We told him that the lists ... (be checked).
We told him that the lists were being checked.

1 They are new employees and haven't started working yet. They ... (be introduced) to the staff.
2 Where is Penny? She is with the personnel manager. She has applied for another position and ... (be interviewed).
3 Follow-on systems ... (be studied) in our research and development department last month when one of the computers caught fire.
4 The new machine is not yet on the market, but it ... (be assembled) in our new production hall.
5 At the moment the XT 800 jets ... (be tested) in our laboratory.
6 There was some trouble with the laser printers. That is why some parts ... (be checked) by the engineers last night.
7 He is waiting at the reception and ... (be offered) a cup of tea.
8 While the new control system ... (be introduced), there was quite a bottleneck at the end of the production line.

Übung 10

In dieser gemischten Übung müssen Sie sich zwischen einfachen und Verlaufsformen des Präsens und des Imperfekts entscheiden.

1 Staff appraisal often . . . (take) the form of a meeting between an employee and his or her line manager.
2 I . . . (think) of the problems of selling in a foreign market: it's not as easy as it appears.
3 Everybody can hear them. They . . . (talk) about some sort of additional pay.
4 A questionnaire . . . (be prepared) to find out whether they would agree to a ban on smoking.
5 Where is she? – She . . . (work) in the store room today.
What . . . (do/she)? – She . . . (count) the audio-tapes.
6 We cannot place an order yet because our chief buyer still . . . (study) the quotations.
7 The computer . . . (be programmed) so we could not check the figures.
8 A contract of employment . . . (contain) details about the job and the pay.
9 He is busy at the moment. He . . . (write) a memo on how to improve the sales team's motivation.
10 The company . . . (want) to increase production.
11 What . . . (do/he) when we called?
12 Why was Tom not here earlier? – He . . . (take) an examination.
13 We always . . . (meet) the target dates for shipment.
14 They think they can penetrate the French market, but I . . . (doubt) whether it is as simple as they believe.
15 We . . . (know) the turnover will be low this year.
16 The meeting was quite tiring. Tony always . . . (raise) objections.
17 Tom often . . . (talk) to Penny. She . . . (find) him rather interesting, too.
18 He cut his hand on the sharp blade while he . . . (replace) it.
19 A good typist . . . (make) few mistakes.
20 Large firms often . . . (set up) holding companies.
21 Susan . . . (work) for Mrs Jenkins, the sales manager. But at the moment she . . . (spend) her holiday on the Mediterranean.
22 He . . . (find) the mistake when he . . . (have) another look at the figures.

Das Perfekt (present perfect)

- Das *present perfect* gibt es in seiner scharf umrissenen Bedeutung im Deutschen nicht. Deshalb gebrauchen wir auch weder die deutsche Bezeichnung (vollendete Gegenwart) noch die lateinische (Perfekt).

- Das *present perfect* verbindet die Vergangenheit mit der Gegenwart.

  We have been in the market for ten years.
  (wir sind jetzt noch dabei)

  We have lost all our customers abroad.
  (wir hatten welche aber haben jetzt keine mehr)

  We have not seen him this week.
  (von Montag bis heute)

- Da das deutsche Perfekt eine Zeit der Vergangenheit ist, das englische *present perfect* aber nicht, gibt es Schwierigkeiten bei der Übersetzung. Man nimmt die Gegenwart und hilft sich mit dem Wörtchen ‚schon' aus.

  We have been market leader for the last ten years.
  (Wir sind schon seit zehn Jahren führend auf dem Markt)

- Das *present perfect* bezeichnet Vorgänge oder Zustände, die zwar schon in der Vergangenheit abgeschlossen wurden, deren Folgen aber noch bis in die Gegenwart reichen.

  He has broken his leg.
  (er humpelt immer noch)

- Das *present perfect* bezeichnet Vorgänge oder Zustände, die in einem noch nicht abgeschlossenen Zeitraum abgeschlossen wurden, wie z.B. *today, this morning, this week* usw.

  He has not had a holiday this year.

- Es gibt Signalwörter, die eine Verbindung zwischen Vergangenheit und Gegenwart herstellen und somit das *present perfect* verlangen. Sie sind eine wichtige Hilfe, wenn man nicht sicher ist, welche Zeit man gebrauchen soll.

  - just (gerade)
    The letters have just been delivered.
  - so far (bis jetzt)
    We have not heard from him so far.
  - not yet (noch nicht)
    They have not yet sent us a quotation.
  - up to now (bis jetzt)
    Up to now we have sold 1000 of them.
  - ever since (seitdem)
    He has been a superb accountant ever since he joined us.
  - never (nie)
    I have never seen such a mess in my life.
  - ever (jemals)
    Have you ever used a video-phone?

Since und for

- Die wichtigsten dieser Signalwörter sind *since* und *for*, die dem Deutschen ‚seit' entsprechen, aber streng voneinander abgegrenzt sind. Man kann im Deutschen für *for* das Wort ‚lang' gebrauchen für *since* nicht.

  - *Since* bezeichnet einen Zeitpunkt, von dem an etwas andauert.
    They have been in Bernhard Street since 1970.
  - *For* bezieht sich auf einen Zeitraum, der schon eine Weile andauert.
    They have been in Bernhard Street for more than 20 years.
    (seit mehr als 20 Jahren)

Übung 11

Setzen Sie entweder since oder for in der Bedeutung von ‚seit' vor die folgenden Ausdrücke.

1. Easter
2. quite a long time
3. centuries
4. the introduction of VAT
5. ages
6. over two months
7. 1958
8. the whole afternoon
9. many weeks
10. 9 o'clock in the morning
11. at least three years
12. breakfast

Übung 12

Ergänzen Sie die Sätze, indem Sie die vorgebenen adverbialen Bestimmungen mit since oder for anschließen.

BEISPIEL   Employees have had to clock in
the firm was established / the last 16 years
Employees have had to clock in since the firm was established.
Employees have had to clock in for the last 16 years.

1. We have not had full employment
the Industrial Revolution / the last hundred years
2. We have used computers to edit documents
they were introduced onto the market / more than 10 years
3. They have not placed any orders with us
two months / we dismissed their complaint
4. In the goods-in department forklifts have been used
the expansion of our production department / 10 years
5. Confidential staff matters have been dealt with at line manager level
the last two years / the merger with Distribution International Ltd.
6. We have had a comfortable seating area in reception
we moved into our new building / at least two years
7. They have exported all over the world
longer than I can remember / the mid-eighties
8. There have been problems with the filing system
the last three months / we gave up ordering the files chronologically

Das present perfect in der Verlaufsform

- Beim Ausdruck von Vorgängen oder Zuständen, die bis in die Gegenwart reichen, stehen die Verben in der Verlaufsform, es sei denn, es handelt sich um solche Verben, die keine Verlaufsform bilden können (*to know, to have, to need, to think, to see* usw., siehe Seite 60).

    I have been typing this huge report for two hours (and I am still doing it).

Übung 13

Setzen Sie die Verben in das einfache present perfect oder in seine Verlaufsform.

BEISPIEL   What . . . (do/you) since you were made redundant?
What have you been doing since you were made redundant?

1. So far their catalogues always . . . (contain) precise information.
2. He . . . (check) the invoices received by the suppliers all morning.
3. Why is he so irritated? – He . . . (query) overdue orders ever since he started work this morning.
4. They . . . (belong) to the McLellan Group since the early sixties.
5. For a long time it . . . (be) his job to check advice notes.
6. They . . . (look) for the mistake for several hours and still . . . (not find) it.
7. She . . . (file) orders, advice notes and invoices ever since she became a filing clerk.
8. There . . . (be) industrial action in some manufacturing industries recently.
9. We . . . (plan) the takeover for the last six months.
10. We . . . (use) always our own standard forms.
11. They . . . (be) on strike for a week now.
12. I . . . (not see) her since she left the company.
13. This week only the electricians . . . (decide) to take strike action.
14. We . . . (agree) to pay cash on delivery.
15. They . . . (be) on a go-slow since Tuesday.
16. The workers . . . (work-to-rule) for more than ten days now.

Das Imperfekt (simple past)

- Das Imperfekt bezieht sich auf in der Vergangenheit abgeschlossene Zustände oder Vorgänge.

  He bought the company.

- Es wird als Erzählzeit der Vergangenheit gebraucht und für schnell aufeinanderfolgende Handlungen.

  He came in, sat down and read the advertisements.

- Es gibt bestimmte Adverbien, die die einfache Vergangenheit verlangen. Damit wird betont, daß die Tatsache zu einem Zeitpunkt in der Vergangenheit abgeschlossen wurde. Zu diesen Signalwörtern, gehören:
  yesterday, last week, die Jahreszahlen, Verbindungen mit *ago,* auch Nebensätze mit *when.*

  She posted that registered letter two weeks ago.

Übung 14

In dieser Übung helfen Ihnen die <u>unterstrichenen</u> Wörter, die korrekte Zeit zu finden: Imperfekt (simple past) oder present perfect.

BEISPIEL At the beginning we ... (not foresee) the immense demand.
At the beginning we did not foresee the immense demand.

1 <u>Last time</u> I ... (telephone) from a phone box.
2 My department ... (call back) <u>just half an hour ago</u>.
3 The catalytic converter greatly ... (reduce) air pollution <u>since its introduction</u>.
4 <u>When I asked him</u> he ... (propose) a short-term investment.
5 <u>The technician was repairing Penny's computer</u> and so she ... (use) a typewriter to do those letters.
6 The cost of living not ... (go up) <u>for three years now</u>.
7 Britain's surplus on invisible earnings ... (go down) <u>since Japan started to dominate the market</u>.

8 The Stock Exchange never . . . (lose) its importance within a modern economy.
9 Share prices . . . (go up) a lot since the end of the big strike.
10 I never . . . (buy) securities with a non-guaranteed rate of interest.
11 When we secured the order from them we . . . (supply) them with all our sales literature.
12 Many years ago we . . . (market) our products ourselves.
13 As it was a late night we . . . (forget) to discuss deliveries.
14 Maintenance . . . (not look) after servicing our products properly since we cut costs.
15 Our turnover . . . (soar) since we took part in the local trade exhibition.

Übung 15

Bilden Sie ganze Sätze und finden Sie die richtige Zeit: Imperfekt (simple past) oder present perfect.

BEISPIEL   we – book – sufficient space on the boat – two months ago
We booked sufficient space on the boat two months ago.

1 last year – they – export – 80% of their production
2 they – sell – only brushes and rollers – so far
3 it's only October and – their turnover – double – this year
4 many orders – come in – in their first year of trading
5 their business – grow – considerably – since then
6 we – have – no letters – today – perhaps some will come by second delivery
7 he – secure – many orders – when he was new at the job
8 we – close – the agreement – last month
9 they – pay – him extra commission – last year
10 she – live – in Belgium – for some years now
11 the products – leave – our factory – last week
12 we – receive – them in good condition – the day before yesterday
13 the goods – reach – our customer – this morning
14 our agents – work – satisfactorily – for us for the last six years
15 we – spend – too much money on market research – in recent years

Übung 16

Beantworten Sie die Fragen, und setzen Sie dabei die Verben in die richtige Zeitform.

BEISPIEL   Have they accepted the conditions?
            Yes, they . . . (accept) them all.
            They . . . (accept) them before Mrs Jenkins left for Turkey.
            Yes, they have accepted them all.
            They accepted them before Mrs Jenkins left for Turkey.

1   Have they offered us new terms?
    Yes, they . . . (offer) us higher trade discounts.
    They . . . (do) so in their letter which we received yesterday.
2   Has he given us the machine for a trial period?
    Yes, he . . . (give) it to us free for six weeks.
    He . . . (give) it to us when he heard that we might buy 20 of them.
3   Do you think they have changed their policy?
    Yes, they . . . (change) their policy when the new managing director took over.
    He . . . (bring in) the changes in the first six months of this year.
4   Have they started their new campaign?
    Yes, they . . . (short form answer).
    They . . . (start) it before the summer sales.
5   Does your sales manager travel much?
    Yes, he . . . (be) to three continents this month.
    And he . . . (travel) to Syria for a week before Christmas.
6   Has your local college ever offered residential courses?
    No, it never . . . (short form answer).
    Many years ago it . . . (decide) they simply didn't pay.
7   Have they increased salaries?
    Yes, they . . . (add) a bonus to basic salaries.
    They . . . (agree) to this a month ago.
8   Have you ever changed your employer?
    Yes, I . . . (short form answer).
    I . . . (change) from Ford to Jaguar last year.

Übung 17

Ordnen Sie die Satzhälften einander zu.

BEISPIEL 1   They have given us a discount of 15%
          2   They gave us a discount of 15%
            a   when we asked for it.
            b   for at least two years.
          Lösung: *1b, 2a*

3   We have sold a lot
4   We sold a lot
    a   last year.
    b   since the beginning of summer.
5   They have launched their new machine, the *Fine Coat S 13*
6   They launched their new machine, the *Fine Coat S 13*
    a   recently.
    b   six months ago.
7   It has been tested
8   It was tested
    a   before sales began.
    b   for a long time.
9   It took us a lot of time
10 It has taken us a lot of time
    a   to find the cause of the trouble.
    b   so far.
11 He charged 15% for his services
12 He has charged 15% for his services
    a   last time.
    b   for as long as I can remember.
13 They have promised to pay a fixed monthly rate
14 They promised to pay a fixed monthly rate
    a   when they signed the contract.
    b   and have done so punctually ever since.
15 She asked me to change some of the terms of the contract
16 She has asked me to change some of the terms of the contract
    a   when I met her at the airport.
    b   several times.

Übung 18

Vervollständigen Sie die Sätze und setzen Sie die Verben in die richtigen Zeitformen (Präsens, present perfect, Imperfekt, einfache und Verlaufsform). Manchmal sind mehrere Lösungen möglich.

1 We always . . . (keep) copies of our orders.
2 He just . . . (join) the firm.
3 She works in the finance department and . . . (control) the day-to-day expenditure.
4 Since spring they . . . (market) their new products aggressively.
5 Our sales . . . (take) a turn for the worse this year.
6 I never . . . (have) the courage to clean the sophisticated machine since it arrived.
7 Tom remembers the day when Penny first . . . (enter) the office.
8 Last week I . . . (be) in trouble because some money was missing.
9 The paper . . . (get) damp. We cannot print on it now.
10 I . . . (buy) the *Financial Times* yesterday, but I . . . (not buy) it today.
11 It is true that she . . . (prove) to us that she is particularly good at handling difficult callers.
12 We only . . . (use) preprinted forms when ordering.
13 We . . . (have) a central filing system for several years.
14 When I . . . (call) the line was engaged.
15 When I wanted to talk to him he . . . (be) busy: he . . . (sort) the mail.
16 He left a message for you and I . . . (put) it on your desk. It must still be there.
17 We . . . (prepare) order forms when they phoned us.
18 We . . . (adopt) new marketing tactics and are now getting on better.
19 I suppose you . . . (hear) how Mrs Jenkins secured the order, did you?
20 They . . . (work) on a commission basis for ever since I can remember.
21 The purchasing manager . . . (have to) sign the forms before they are collected.
22 He . . . (decide) what duties he wants to delegate.
23 We . . . (look for) premises, large enough to display all our goods, but we . . . (not be) successful so far.
24 We know they . . . (take up) bankers' references at the moment so all we can do now is wait.

Die Konditionalsätze (if-Sätze)

Einführung

- Konditionalsätze sind Nebensätze, die hauptsächlich mit den Wörtern *if, if not* oder *unless* eingeleitet werden. Sie heißen auch *if*-Sätze oder auch Bedingungssätze, weil sie eine Bedingung nennen, die sich auf das Geschehen im Hauptsatz bezieht.

  If you sign the contract,   *we shall start working tomorrow.*
  Bedingung im Nebensatz   Geschehen im Hauptsatz

- Ein *if*-Satz kann vor oder nach einem Hauptsatz stehen.

  If it rains, we shall postpone it. We shall postpone it if it rains.

- Im Deutschen sind grammatisch korrekte Konditionalsätze wegen des richtigen Gebrauchs des Konjunktivs bzw. des Imperfekts und der entsprechenden *würde*-Formen, die nicht doppelt vorkommen sollen, ziemlich schwierig.
  Im Englischen haben Sie es wesentlich einfacher.

- Es gibt drei Typen von *if-Sätzen*, die als feste Konstruktionen im Sprachgebrauch vorkommen und die hier erklärt werden.

    ◊ **Typ 1:** Bedingung erfüllbar
    If we mail the letter today, they will have it tomorrow.
    If I get the job, I will buy a bigger car.

    ◊ **Typ 2:** Bedingung zweifelhaft oder imaginär
    If we mailed the letter today, they would have it tomorrow.
    If I were a millionaire, I would stop working.

    ◊ **Typ 3:** Es hätte etwas geschehen können, doch die Bedingung ist nicht erfüllt worden.
    If we had mailed the letter, they would have had it tomorrow.
    If I had moved to Leeds, I would have got the job.

- Daraus ergibt sich folgendes grammatisches Schema:

	If-Satz	**Hauptsatz**
Typ 1	Präsens If I get the job,	Futur 1 I will buy a bigger car.
Typ 2	Imperfekt If I were a millionaire,	Konditional 1 I would stop working.
Typ 3	Plusquamperfekt If I had moved to Leeds,	Konditional 2 I would have got the job.

- Im *if*-Satz stehen (fast) nie Formen von *shall/will* oder *should/would*.
- Vorangestellte *if*-Sätze werden vom Hauptsatz durch ein Komma getrennt.

Übung 1

Verbinden Sie die beiden Sätze, und achten Sie auf den in Klammern angegebenen Typ. Beginnen Sie jeweils mit If.

BEISPIEL You have a computer. You find your work more fun. (Typ 2)
If you had a computer, you would find your work more fun.

1 You read the instructions. You know how to handle the machine. (Typ 1)
2 We publish regular newsletters for our employees. Our staff is better informed about our activities. (Typ 3)
3 You are a computer expert. You have many jobs open to you. (Typ 2)
4 You pass the entrance examination. You are able to register for the course. (Typ 2)
5 They modernize their equipment. I stay with the company. (Typ 3)
6 Companies install video-conferencing facilities. It allows the participants of a meeting to see and hear each other in conference rooms all over the world. (Typ 2)
7 You are the cheapest supplier. You get the order. (Typ 3)
8 You work hard. You get to the top. (Typ 1)

9 You have good references. You get the job. (Typ 3)
10 You speak English fluently. You get a better job. (Typ 1)
11 I get a good offer. I accept it. (Typ 3)
12 I have better computer skills. I apply for more interesting jobs. (Typ 2)
13 Microcomputers are built into credit cards. It revolutionizes the methods used to transfer and borrow money. (Typ 2)
14 We have more open discussions. We avoid several misunderstandings. (Typ 3)
15 We have better management/staff relations. It increases motivation and improve efficiency. (Typ 3)

Übung 2

Sie haben drei Typen von Konditionalsätzen kennengelernt. Bilden Sie die zwei anderen Formen.

BEISPIEL   If you give us their address, we will ask them for a quotation.
If you gave us their address, we would ask them for a quotation.
If you had given us their address, we would have asked them for a quotation.

1 If the pattern had had our customers' approval, we would have placed a substantial order.
2 If you sent us a dozen of them on approval, we would test the demand for them.
3 If we are not under pressure, there will not be any mistakes.
4 If there is a friendly atmosphere, work will be more efficient.
5 He will not leave the company if promotion prospects improve.
6 If the company employed younger executives, it would probably benefit from their new ideas.
7 If he has some knowledge of export procedures, he will get the job.
8 If they had clear managerial objectives, their business would improve.
9 He would be the right man for us if he adopted a more analytical approach.
10 We would have taken her on if she had applied for the job.
11 If you write his name clearly, the letter will be delivered without delay.
12 If they had sent a cheque in time, they would not have received a reminder.

Übung 3

Setzen Sie die folgenden Sätze in alle drei Formen möglicher Konditional-Konstruktionen, wobei Sie die in Klammern gegebenen Verben benutzen.

BEISPIEL If I ... (need) peace and quiet, I ... (shut myself) in my office.
If I need peace and quiet, I will shut myself in my office.
If I needed peace and quiet, I would shut myself in my office.
If I had needed peace and quiet, I would have shut myself in my office.

1 I ... (book) a seat if they ... (have) a place available on flight BA 608.
2 If the prices of your products ... (be) reasonable, we ... (place) a trial order.
3 If our new range ... (sell) well, we ... (increase) production.
4 We ... (not lose) the customer if we ... (keep) in touch.
5 I ... (tell) you if I ... (have) the exact sales figures.
6 We ... (find) the mistake easily if we ... (run through) the figures again.
7 If he ... (want) to work for us, he ... (need) to change his attitude.
8 They ... (save) a lot of money if they ... (arrange) telephone conferences.
9 If you ... (want) to come on Friday, that ... (be) fine with us.
10 If something else ... (come up) at the last minute, I ... (tell) you.

Übung 4

Vervollständigen Sie die vorgegebenen Konditional-Strukturen mit den entsprechenden Formen von Typ 3.

BEISPIELE What ... (do/you) if they had cancelled the contract?
What would you have done if ...
If they ... (insist), we would have paid.
If they had insisted, we would have paid.

1 If they ... (pass) the delivery note on to me, we would have paid.
2 We ... (contact) you earlier if we had seen your advertisement.
3 If we had seen that our stock was running low, we ... (re-order).

4 We would have placed an order if your prices ... (be) lower.
5 If we had not been confined to the domestic market, we ... (do) much better.
6 If we ... (not meet) the deadline, we would have faced a £20,000 penalty.
7 He ... (not give up) on the job if his boss had not asked him to.
8 If he had not reorganized his time, he ... (not get) on top of his work.
9 The campaign would have been more successful if they ... (broadcast) their commercials in prime time.
10 We ... (finish) it if we had not been interrupted so often.
11 If the frying pan had not been so hot, the tablecloth ... (not catch) fire.
12 If she ... (give) the Board a clear picture of her sales performance, there would not have been any misunderstandings.

Übung 5

Vervollständigen Sie die vorgegebenen Konditional-Strukturen mit der passenden Zeitstufe.

BEISPIEL If we do not face up to competition, we ... (be) in trouble soon.
If we do not face up to competition, we will be in trouble soon.

1 If I had to travel to the USA, I ... (choose) to go by Concorde.
2 If you ... (not provide) sales literature without spelling mistakes, your customers will not take your products seriously.
3 If we had been informed in time, we ... (take) measures to protect ourselves from potential losses.
4 If your machines ... (prove) satisfactory, we will install them in all our shops.
5 We would buy a new system, if the computer market ... (not be) changing so rapidly.
6 If the sales figures indicate that the market is saturated, we ... (change) our range of products.
7 We ... (save) a lot of time if the employees were served a cup of tea at their desks instead of making it themselves.
8 If they don't take the faulty goods back, we ... (place) the matter in the hands of our solicitors.
9 I ... (not keep) you so long if I had known you were busy.

10 If he ... (talk) to me like that, I would have resigned.
11 I ... (call) back immediately if I had had time.
12 What ... (happen) if we held board meetings only once a month?
13 If you are selected, you ... (get) a good salary with bonuses.
14 If staff had to be made redundant, the usual procedure ... (be) "last in, first out".

Übung 6

Bilden Sie Konditionalsätze, indem Sie die Formen von if ... had not (done) und would not have (done) verwenden.

BEISPIEL   Tom attended the training course. He met our new agent there.
If Tom had not attended the training course, he would not have met our new agent there.

1 We kept an eye on them. They continued their work.
2 The company provided good service. It earned itself a good reputation.
3 He was often late for work. They checked his attendance record.
4 We were so strict with the staff. We got into trouble with the sales manager.
5 We studied the regional sales figures. We learned about the dramatic decline in North-East England.
6 I showed the bank manager our business plan. He granted us a loan.
7 They worked overtime. They sorted out the technical problems.
8 The new boss set new standards and targets. The company beat all their competitors.
9 She selected the people carefully. She found the right person for the job.
10 They set up an internal Assessment Centre. They identified talented staff for management positions in their own company.
11 We advertised for a new office manager. We had problems with the secretarial staff.
12 The stockmarket was behaving a bit strangely. I sold most of my shares.
13 The machines were serviced regularly. They performed well.
14 The fog at Heathrow was so terrible. The plane was delayed.

Der Gebrauch von was und were im if-Satz

♦ Im *if*-Satz steht häufig noch im Imperfekt die Form *were* und nicht *was*. Das ist das einzige Überbleibsel des alten Konjunktivs im Englischen (*were* = wäre). Allerdings hat in der Umgangssprache bereits das *was* die Form *were* weitgehend verdrängt, besonders in Zusammenhang mit *I*. Beide Formen sind korrekt.

If I was/were a millionaire, I would not work any more.
If I was/were you, I'd apply for another job.

Übung 7

Formulieren Sie den zweiten Satz um und beginnen Sie mit If I was/ were you.

BEISPIEL   They are well prepared for a strike. Give in to some of their demands.
If I was/were you, I would give in to some of their demands.

1 There are some vacancies in that firm. Write a letter of application.
2 Being in a partnership always reduces risks. Look for one or two experienced business people in your line of work.
3 You are looking for competitive exchange rates? Try one of the high street banks.
4 It is understandable that you want to see the completed plans as soon as possible. Just ask him to send them by fax.
5 You wonder why your sales figures are poor? Rethink your sales strategy and become more customer-orientated.
6 You say that the quality of the T-shirts comes up to your expectations. Place a big order before the season starts and profit from a bulk discount.
7 You find answering all the enquiries too time-consuming? Have a leaflet or price-list printed.
8 You want to find out what their terms are? Ask them for their catalogue.
9 They offer even small quantities at competitive prices. Tell them you are interested in their catalogue.
10 On Malta they drive on the left. Do not rent a car there.

11 It really doesn't matter if you have lost your plane ticket because your name can be checked on the computer. Just go to your airline's check-in desk.
12 You are not satisfied in your present job? Look for a vacancy in another company.
13 You don't know what to do to attract more customers? Open a cafeteria which also serves vegetarian food.
14 I gather a lot of time is wasted by your staff making coffee. Install an automatic coffee machine.
15 You don't think you can be home on Friday evening? Go to the airport and get on stand-by.

Übung 8

Setzen Sie die in Klammern stehenden Verben in die richtige Zeitform.

BEISPIEL   If his attendance were 100%, he ... (get) a cash bonus.
If his attendance were 100%, he would get a cash bonus.

1 If we took the middle-aged candidate, it ... (be) a problem.
2 If he ... (not increase) the pay offer, the union representatives will not accept it.
3 There would have been trouble if we ... (not renegotiate) the redundancy payments.
4 Distribution costs will be reduced if the new warehouse ... (be) completed on time.
5 If they ... (decide) to ignore our recommendations, it would be disastrous.
6 If our distribution had been handled by an agent, it ... (be) the wrong way to do business in that particular country.
7 If we ... (set up) our own sales organisation in this developing country, it would fail because we do not have enough local contacts.
8 Someone else will penetrate that expanding market if we ... (not do) so.
9 We ... (lose) our chance if we had waited any longer.
10 If we appointed an agent for a short time, at least it ... (be) an attempt to get a foothold in the market.

Die unvollständigen Hilfsverben im if-Satz

◆ Umschreibungsformen der unvollständigen Hilfsverben sind möglich, jedoch werden komplizierte Formen *(they will not have been able to, they would have had to)* häufig vermieden.

Eine Tabelle zeigt, wie stark vereinfacht werden kann:

können	
Typ 1	will be able → can If there is an emergency, she can go home.
Typ 2	would be able → could If there were an emergency, she could go home.
Typ 3	would have been able → could have If there had been an emergency, she could have gone home.
dürfen	
Typ 1	will be allowed → may If there is an emergency, she may go home.
Typ 2	would be allowed → might If there were an emergency, she might go home.
Typ 3	would have been allowed → might have If there had been an emergency, she might have gone home.
müssen	
Typ 1	will have to → must If our sales rise, we must have additional space for stock.

Übung 9

In dieser gemischten Übung setzen Sie vereinfachte Formen (can, must, could, might) statt der Umschreibungsformen (be able, be allowed to, have to) ein.

BEISPIELE If we had employed an agent, he ... (can) sort it out for us.
... *he could have sorted it out for us.*
If we do not finish the new pricelist, we ... (must) go in to work on Sunday.
... *we must go in to work on Sunday.*

1 If we had had more time, we ... (can) finish the plan by the end of the week.
2 He will go out of his mind if I ... (not can) find the insurance policy.
3 If he wants to see better results, he ... (must) get his people to work as a team.
4 She ... (not can) do a good job if she constantly has to work under pressure.
5 If we do not finish the project, we ... (not may) go on leave.
6 If the spare parts are not available, we ... (must) replace the machines.
7 We ... (must) be prepared for several years of low profits if we take this course of action.
8 If the train is delayed, we ... (not can) have a cup of tea before the meeting.
9 If there are no applications, we ... (must) advertise the vacant jobs again.
10 You ... (can) stop the machine by pressing the red button if there were an emergency.
11 He ... (may) go to the conference if he finishes his report.
12 If we employed more sales representatives, we ... (can) beat our competitors.
13 If we take on more staff, we ... (must) extend our canteen.
14 If we had been informed in time, we ... (can) deal with it immediately.
15 If they don't pay, we ... (must) send them a reminder.
16 If you had ordered this with us, you ... (can) exchange it.

Übung 10

Vervollständigen Sie die Sätze und setzen Sie das in Klammern stehende Verb in die richtige Form des Passivs.

BEISPIEL   If you insist on fast payment, settlement by banker's draft . . . (be arranged).
If you insist on fast payment, settlement by banker's draft will be arranged.

1 If the installation . . . (be finished) by the end of March, we would be able to start production by mid-April.
2 If I had chosen a non-guaranteed rate of interest, part of my profit . . . (be lost).
3 We could have developed new training programmes if a new personnel manager . . . (be appointed).
4 If we want insurance cover, protective clothing . . . (must be worn).
5 If our delivery is a week late, claims for compensation . . . (be made).
6 Even if freight-free delivery . . . (be agreed upon), shipment would have been at the customer's expense.
7 If you were a customer with our bank, a cheque card . . . (can be issued).
8 If more computers were installed, more jobs . . . (be lost).
9 If staff have to be made redundant, men and women between 50-65 . . . (be selected).
10 If overdrafts can only be obtained at high interest rates, banks . . . (be asked) for loans by fewer people.
11 If I . . . (be asked) where to invest money, I would suggest the computer software industry.
12 If I went to a broker, my money . . . (be invested) wisely.

Übung 11

In dieser Übung sind die korrekten Verbformen zu finden und einzusetzen. Die Sätze beziehen sich auf das Versicherungswesen.

BEISPIEL   If you needed general information, you ... (can) find it in an insurance prospectus.
If you needed general information, you could find it in an insurance prospectus.

1. If you ... (have) a credit insurance, bad debts will be covered.
2. If you have a no claims discount (NCD), your insurance premium ... (be reduced).
3. Even if the claimant himself is to blame for the accident, the damage caused to his own car ... (be covered) by his 'comprehensive' insurance.
4. If I had to take out insurance, I ... (contact) a broker.
5. If you are sure about the type of insurance you want, you ... (be asked) to complete a proposal form.
6. If you ... (not tell) the truth when completing the proposal form, your insurance cover may be declared void.
7. If you wanted to insure a risk that would not result in your suffering a financial loss, the insurance company ... (not accept) your proposal.
8. If you want to know the full terms of insurance, you ... (must) read the policy.
9. Insurance cover would lapse if you ... (not pay) premiums on time.
10. If there is a loss, the policyholder ... (must) fill in a form to make a claim.

Die modalen Hilfsverben

Einführung

- Hilfsverben können nicht alleine stehen, z.B. die Aussage ‚Er soll' ist unsinnig, wenn man nicht weiß, was er ‚soll'. Hilfsverben verhelfen einem anderen Verb zu einer richtigen Aussage: ‚Er soll lernen.' Man nennt sie auch *modale Hilfsverben,* weil sie ein anderes Verb näher bestimmen (modifizieren): Er ‚soll, darf, muß, kann, will' arbeiten.

- Die meisten dieser modalen Hilfsverben können im Englischen nicht in alle Zeitformen gesetzt werden (z.B. *must* gibt es nur im Präsens, *can* nur im Präsens und Imperfekt). Deshalb heißen sie auch *unvollständige Hilfsverben.* Das Englische weicht in diesen Fällen bei der Bildung anderer Zeitformen auf Umschreibungen aus: *can = to be able; must = to have to.*

- Schließlich gibt es einige Verben, die sowohl als Vollverben wie auch als Hilfsverben auftreten können *(do, have, dare, need)*, was oft zu fehlerhaftem Sprachgebrauch Anlaß gibt. Denn Hilfsverben sind im Gegensatz zu Vollverben definiert als Verben, die

    ◇ in Frage und Verneinung nicht mit *to do* umschrieben werden:
    May I come in?
    We cannot help you.

    ◇ kein *s* in der 3. Person Singular Präsens haben:
    He must go.

    ◇ den Infinitiv des folgenden Verbs ohne *to* anschließen (Ausnahme: *ought to*):
    We should work now.

Können, Möglichkeit, Erlaubnis
(can/could, to be able to)

- *Can* (Ersatzform: *to be able to*) bezeichnet hauptsächlich eine geistige oder körperliche Fähigkeit.

  He has been able to collect them.

- Die Verneinungsformen sind *cannot (can't), could not (couldn't)*.

  She could not come to the interview.

- Die Verneinung des Ersatzverbs erfolgt ganz normal mit *not*.

  We are not able to deliver.

- Ersatzformen von *can*:

Präsens	*am able to* ...	ich kann ...
Imperfekt	*was able to* ...	ich konnte ...
Perfekt	*have been able to* ...	ich habe ... können
Plusqu.	*had been able to* ...	ich hatte ... können
Futur 1	*I will be able to* ...	ich werde ... können
Kond. 1	*I should/would be able to* ...	ich würde ... können
Kond. 2	*I should/would have been able to* ...	ich hätte ... können

- Wie im Deutschen kann *can* eine Erlaubnis und eine Möglichkeit ausdrücken.

  You can have my typewriter today.

- *Can/could* werden bei einer höflichen Bitte oder einem Vorschlag verwendet.

  Can you ring him up for me, please?
  Could we not stop the whole project?

Übung 1

Setzen Sie die folgenden Sätze in die in Klammern angegebenen Zeitformen mit den entsprechenden Umschreibungsformen von to be able to.

BEISPIEL We cannot understand the meaning. (Fut. 1, Plusqu.)
We will not be able to understand the meaning.
We had not been able to understand the meaning.

1 Everybody can fill in our new questionnaire. (Fut. 1, Perf.)
2 You cannot despatch the goods on time. (Imp., Kond. 2)
3 We can buy them in bulk at moderate prices. (Fut. 1, Kond. 2)
4 We can clear up the matter. (Fut. 1)
5 They cannot afford a bigger shop. (Perf., Kond. 1)
6 He can get a ticket for the Trade Fair in Moscow. (Kond. 1, Plusqu.)
7 They can increase their turnover. (Imp.)
8 Because of the lack of raw materials, we cannot keep up with our continental competitors. (Perf.)
9 We cannot ship the goods by air. (Plusqu.)
10 We cannot develop a new product in such a short time. (Imp.)

Übung 2

Setzen Sie passende Zeitformen von can oder to be able to in die Lücken.

BEISPIEL If you open a current account, you must learn how to complete a paying-in slip, otherwise you ... (not) pay cash into your own account.
... you will not (won't) be able to pay ...

1 If you have a current account, you ... use cheques for making payments.
2 First you open a current account, then you ... withdraw money whenever you want.
3 He arranged credit facilities and so he ... overdraw his account.
4 We had a current account, so we ... make payments by standing order.
5 If he had had a current account, his employer ... pay his salary into his account by credit transfer.

6   She has no current account. If she had, she . . . arrange regular payments by direct debit.
7   Only current account holders . . . withdraw cash from cash dispensing machines.
8   You don't have to go to your own bank's 'hole in the wall'. You . . . go to any cash dispenser if you need money.

Erlaubnis, Möglichkeit, Verbot (may, might, to be allowed to, must not)

♦   *May (might)* bezeichnen hauptsächlich eine Erlaubnis oder eine Bitte, etwas tun zu dürfen. In diesem Sinne gebraucht man im Präsens *may* (eher formal). *May* wird immer mehr verdrängt und durch *can* ersetzt.

— *May I come in?*
— *Might I propose an alteration to that clause in the contract?*

♦   Ein allgemeines Verbot wird meist mit *must not* ausgesprochen.

You must not smoke here.

♦   Wie im Deutschen kann man mit *may* auch eine Möglichkeit ausdrücken.

— *He may not be in his office.*
— *He might have left already.*

♦   Alle Zeiten können mit *to be allowed to* (auch *to be permitted to*) gebildet werden.

We are always allowed to ask questions.

- Die Verneinung des Ersatzverbs erfolgt ganz normal mit *not*.

  We are not (aren't) allowed to export weapons to certain countries.

- Ersatzformen von *may*:

Präsens	I am allowed to . . .	ich darf . . .
Imperfekt	I was allowed to . . .	ich durfte . . .
Perfekt	I have been allowed to . . .	ich habe . . . dürfen
Plusqu.	I had been allowed to . . .	ich hatte . . . dürfen
Futur 1	I will be allowed to . . .	ich werde . . . dürfen
Kond. 1	I should/would be allowed to . . .	ich würde . . . dürfen
Kond. 2	I should/would have been allowed to . . .	ich hätte dürfen

Übung 3

In den folgenden Sätzen finden Sie Hilfsverben im Präsens. Aufgabe ist es, sie durch die Umschreibungsformen in den in Klammern angegeben Zeitstufen zu ersetzen.

BEISPIEL She must not leave the office before 4 o'clock. (Fut. 1)
She will not (won't) be allowed to leave the office before 4 o'clock.

1. He must not take over the sales department. (Fut. 1)
2. He must not drink beer on the compound. (Imp.)
3. They must not copy our logo. (Imp., Perf.)
4. I may rent a car there. (Kond. 1)
5. We must not cooperate with them. (Fut. 1)
6. They must not export them without a licence. (Präs., Perf.)
7. You must not withdraw large sums without prior notice. (Kond. 1)
8. You must not deliver them on a Bank Holiday. (Fut. 1)
9. They must not sell without authorisation. (Kond. 2, Präs.)
10. We must not advertise in national papers. (Imp., Plusqu.)

Übung 4

Vervollständigen Sie die Sätze durch Formen von may/might, must not oder deren Umschreibungen. Manchmal sind mehrere Lösungen möglich.

BEISPIEL   The goods sold must be as described. A shirt described as blue ... (not) turn out to be lilac.
A shirt described as blue must not turn out to be lilac.

1 Consumers buying goods or services ... (not) be exploited.
2 There is a possibility that the incorrect weight or quantity ... have been given.
3 Goods ... have been incorrectly labelled by mistake.
4 Firms ... (not) consult each other in order to keep prices high.
5 Consumer legislation offers protection through Acts of Parliament. People who sell goods are told what they may do and what they ... (not) do.
6 You ... sue the seller if goods supplied are faulty and if he refuses to replace the items or give you a refund.
7 A salesperson ... (not) give a customer false information about a product.
8 A friend of mine recently started selling food in an old barn. She ... (not) continue now that Environmental Health Officers have stated that the place is not clean enough.
9 I hear somebody you know wants to sell prepacked meat. Well, he ... (not) do so unless the labelling on each individual packet clearly shows the weight.
10 Advertisers ... (not) deviate from the Advertising Standards Authority guidelines which make sure advertising is fair.

Übung 5

In dieser gemischten Übung setzen Sie die in Klammern angegebenen Verbformen in die passende Zeitform ein. Gelegentlich sind zwei Lösungen möglich.

BEISPIEL Ms Walker recently appointed two supervisors, because she simply ... (not be able to) oversee the day-to-day administration of the department on her own.
... was not able to ...

1 According to the latest directive from the Board we ... (may not) give any cash bonuses to our agents for the next six months.
2 To improve sales I suggested that we spent more on advertising, but the Board said that we ... (can not) do that.
3 The amount of industrial waste has fallen rapidly to only five tons a month. Do you think we ... (can) reduce it any further? (zwei Lösungen möglich)
4 You know about his difficulties here. I am sending him to a small branch in the north. I hope that he ... (can) fit in better there.
5 Before we gave him the job we checked his application carefully. We think he ... (can) fill the vacancy in R & D perfectly.
6 If there is another serious mistake, he ... (may) find himself answerable to the Board.
7 Did you try to find out what is wrong with him? I'm afraid his colleagues ... (to be not able to) accept him. (zwei Lösungen möglich)
8 The leader of our negotiating team has a personal problem at the moment. His wife is asking for a divorce and he is terribly upset about it. So it is possible that he ... (may not) represent the company in the coming negotiations.
9 I advised my boss to look for an alternative supplier but I ... (can not) convince him.
10 It was not necessary to bring up the point about a sale or return agreement. Our customers ... (can) always return goods within a reasonable time-frame.

Zwang, Notwendigkeit (must, have to)

- Im Präsens stehen im Aussagesatz drei Formen für das deutsche ‚müssen' zur Wahl:

  > must
  > to have to
  > to have got to

  Alle drei drücken einen Zwang, Befehl, eine Anordnung, Anweisung, Verpflichtung oder ein Gebot aus (*to have got to* wird nur im Präsens gebraucht).

- Das unvollständige Hilfsverb *must* gibt es nur im Präsens.

- Die Formen für das Präsens können auch für das Futur gebraucht werden.

- Mögliche Formen in den anderen Zeiten:

Präsens	*We must pay in cash. We have (got) to pay in cash.* Wir müssen in bar bezahlen.
Imperfekt	*We had to pay in cash.* Wir mußten in bar bezahlen.
Perfekt	*We have had to pay in cash.* Wir haben in bar bezahlen müssen.
Plusqu.	*We had had to pay in cash.* Wir hatten in bar bezahlen müssen.
Futur 1	*We will have to pay in cash.* Wir werden in bar bezahlen müssen.
Kond. 1	*We would have to pay in cash.* Wir würden in bar bezahlen müssen.
Kond. 2	*We would have had to pay in cash.* Wir hätten in bar bezahlen müssen.

Übung 6

Setzen Sie die gegebenen Sätze in die in Klammern angegebenen Zeitformen. (Sie können in dieser Übung die entsprechenden Formen von to have to verwenden.)

BEISPIEL   He must take it back. (Imp.)
   He had to take it back.

1 We must agree to their conditions. (Imp.)
2 He has to notify Mr Reade. (Kond. 1)
3 I have to type the memos before the weekend. (Fut. 1)
4 They must make concessions. (Fut. 1)
5 We had to come to an agreement. (Fut. 1)
6 They will have to overcome their difficulties first. (Imp.)
7 He must give up his position. (Kond. 1)
8 They had to use the loan to safeguard jobs. (Fut. 1)
9 Working conditions on the shop floor must be improved. (Imp.)
10 You must aim to improve on last year's sales. (Fut. 1)
11 We must attach a pro forma invoice to the despatch note. (Imp.)
12 The information sheet must be distributed before the meeting. (Imp.)
13 We must translate the letter to them into German. (Kond. 1)
14 The postcode must be written directly after the address. (Präs.)

Übung 7

Bilden Sie Satzpaare, indem Sie der ersten Satzhälfte die passende zweite Satzhälfte zuordnen. Es gibt jeweils nur eine Möglichkeit.

BEISPIEL   I can see you have little time at the moment, but
   a   we will have to answer the letter at once.
   b   we have had to answer the letter at once.
   c   we would have to answer the letter at once.
   Lösung: *a*

1 The contract has finally been agreed upon, but I'm afraid
   a   you must type it again.
   b   you had to type it again.
   c   you would have to type it again.

2 I think they managed to understand your talk,
   a   but you had to send them all a summary.
   b   but you must send them all a summary.
   c   but you would have to send them all a summary.
3 If we accepted their order,
   a   we must cut supplies to our local customers.
   b   we had to cut supplies to our local customers.
   c   we would have to cut supplies to our local customers.
4 I think we need new ones
   a   although we would then have to throw out the old ones.
   b   although we would then must throw out the old ones.
   c   although we would then have had to throw out the old ones.
5 There was a strict penalty clause and
   a   that's why we must meet the deadline.
   b   that's why we must have met the deadline.
   c   that's why we had to meet the deadline.
6 Soon they will be out of date
   a   so we must invest some money in R & D.
   b   so we had to invest some money in R & D.
   c   so we would have to invest some money in R & D.
7 The fair lasted for ten days, and
   a   she has to stay there the whole time.
   b   she had to stay there the whole time.
   c   she would have to stay there the whole time.
8 One important part is missing,
   a   I'm afraid we will have to tell the supervisor.
   b   I'm afraid we would have to tell the supervisor.
   c   I'm afraid we had to tell the supervisor.
9 If you got the job,
   a   you will have to work hard.
   b   you had got to work hard.
   c   you would have to work hard.
10 We have too much absenteeism
   a   so we must take a tougher line with our staff.
   b   so we would have to take a tougher line with our staff.
   c   so we would have had to take a tougher line with our staff.

Der verneinte Zwang
(don't have to, need not, don't need to)

- Die möglichen Formen des ‚Nicht-Brauchens', die in ihrer Bedeutung beliebig austauschbar sind, sind:

Präsens	I needn't come I don't need to come I don't have to come	Ich brauche nicht zu kommen.
Imp.	I didn't need to come I didn't have to come	Ich brauchte nicht zu kommen.
Futur 1	I won't need to come I won't have to come	Ich werde nicht zu kommen brauchen. Es wird nicht nötig sein, daß ich komme.

- *Need* kann sowohl als Vollverb mit Umschreibung und Anschluß des Infinitivs mit *to* gebraucht werden *(didn't need to come)* als auch als Hilfsverb ohne Umschreibung mit *to do* und mit direktem Anschluß des Infinitivs *(needn't come)*.

Übung 8

Alle Sätze in dieser Übung sind im Präsens. Beantworten Sie die Fragen mit der Kurzform, und gebrauchen Sie alle drei möglichen Formen des ‚Nicht-Brauchens'.

BEISPIEL Do the representatives have to pay for accommodation?
No, they needn't.
No, they don't need to.
No, they don't have to.

1 Do we need to replace the old machines this year?
2 Do you have to consult the MD on every day problems?
3 Do they need to expand their operation in Asia?
4 Do we have to pay for the goods we have on trial at once?
5 Do you have to pay for insurance?

6   Do employees have to ask for an increase in salary in this company?
7   Must we send our order today?
8   Must the members of the staff pay for the tickets?
9   Must we agree on the terms right now?
10 Do I have to ask them for the financial standing of every customer?

Übung 9

Setzen Sie die folgenden Sätze in die angegebene Zeit. Verwenden Sie don't have to.

BEISPIEL   We need not retype it. (Imp.)
           We didn't have to retype it.

1   I need not work on Saturday next year. (Fut. 1)
2   We will not have to buy them in big quantities. (Kond. 1)
3   Mrs Jenkins need not fly to Paris after all. (Fut. 1)
4   They do not have to settle all their invoices before the end of the month. (Imp.)
5   He will not have to attend the meeting. (Präs.)
6   They do not have to confirm this order in writing. (Fut. 1)
7   We need not take his advice. (Imp.)
8   They won't have to pay in advance. (Präs.)

Zwei schwierigere Formen des verneinten Zwanges (did not have to und need not have)

— ♦ *I did not have to go immediately.*
    Ich brauchte nicht sofort zu gehen (und ging auch nicht sofort).

— ♦ *I need not have gone immediately.*
    Ich hätte nicht sofort zu gehen brauchen (aber ich tat es trotzdem, weil ich es nicht wußte).

Übung 10

Setzen Sie eine der angegebenen Formen (did not have to, need not have) ein, so daß die Sätze einen Sinn bekommen. In einigen Fällen gibt es zwei Möglichkeiten.

BEISPIELE You (give) ... me another ring, I was already on my way
You need not have given me another ring, I was already on my way.
To his relief he heard that he (explain) ... to Mr Reade himself, Mrs Jenkins had already done so.
To his relief he heard that he did not have to explain to Mr Reade, Mrs Jenkins had already done so.

1 We ... (spend) more on advertising because these products sold very well in Asia anyway.
2 Tom ... (write) the minutes. He would not have liked to do so.
3 They ... (make) a claim. The money was already credited to their account.
4 Fortunately we ... (complete) this order immediately, so we were able to supply other customers first.
5 We ... (pay) in cash, but we did and we got a considerable discount for doing so.
6 He ... (tell) me because I had already got instructions from my own department.
7 You ... (worry) about your business, your competitors did not even get planning permission for the new building.
8 We ... (change) our supplier after all, which saved us a lot of trouble.
9 You ... (try) so often to get through, the line was dead this morning.
10 We ... (pay) a fine in the end, the affair was settled by arbitration.
11 They ... (hurry), they had two more weeks before delivery.
12 You ... (send) a dispatch note, but we were glad you did.
13 He ... (pay) for his railway ticket himself. The company pays all travelling expenses.
14 We ... (send) a new request for payment. They had just mislaid the original invoice.
15 They ... (worry) about the packaging. We had agreed on transportation in containers.

Verbot und verneinter Zwang (must not, need not)

- *Must not* bezeichnet im Gegensatz zum Deutschen („muß nicht") ein Verbot.

  You must not open the photocopier if it is still plugged in. You could get a shock.

- *Need not* drückt aus, daß keine Notwendigkeit besteht, etwas zu tun.

  You needn't do these letters today. They are not urgent.

Übung 11

Setzen Sie must not oder need not in die Lücken ein, so daß sich ein Sinn ergibt.

BEISPIEL   You . . . give me a ring. I'll come and see you in any case.
You need not give me a ring. I'll come and see you in any case.

1   You . . . forget to type the report.
2   We . . . disturb him when he is in a meeting.
3   She is very capable and so . . . go on another training course.
4   You . . . type the letter today, tomorrow will do.
5   You . . . smoke in an office you share with a non-smoker.
6   You . . . make a note of every point he makes.
7   You . . . have your lunch in the canteen if you don't want to.
8   Employees . . . park their cars in the visitors' carpark.
9   You . . . lose your temper even if your customer does.
10 We . . . file the correspondence twice a day, once will do.
11 We . . . go back any further. He only opened an account with us a year ago.
12 You . . . criticize a product that you are not familiar with.
13 You . . . argue with an angry customer even if you think that he is wrong.
14 It's OK, you . . . turn on the light yet. We can see quite well.
15 They . . . talk during the examination.

Die Frage nach einem Zwang oder einer Notwendigkeit

- Die möglichen Formen der Frage nach einem Zwang oder einer Notwendigkeit sind:

Präsens	Do I have to come?, Need I come?, Do I need to come?, Have I got to come?, Must I come?
Imp.	Did I have to come?, Did I need to come?
Futur 1	Will I have to come?, Will I need to come?

- Verwenden Sie am besten grundsätzlich die Formen von *to have to* mit Umschreibung:

  Do we have to come?

Übung 12

Setzen Sie die gegebenen Aussagesätze in die Frageform und verwenden Sie dabei to have to.

BEISPIEL   He clocks out when he goes home for lunch.
Does he have to clock out when he goes home for lunch?

1   We keep all their letters.
2   He will order new stationery.
3   We accept foreign coins.
4   She translates the quotations.
5   You are late.
6   We paid compensation.
7   He complains so much.
8   He repaired the coffee machine.
9   They will wait outside.
10   We ask for a pay rise.
11   We cancelled the agreement.
12   They will replace the calculators.

Sollen (shall, should, ought to, to be supposed to)

- *Shall* wird sowohl verwendet, um einen Vorschlag oder ein Angebot zu machen als auch, um eine Bitte auszudrücken.

    Shall we ask them for a discount?
    Sollen wir sie um einen Rabatt bitten?

- *Should* drückt einen Rat oder eine Verpflichtung aus (*should* = sollte, *should have* = hätte sollen). Eine noch stärkere Verpflichtung wird durch *ought to* (= sollte eigentlich und ist nur in dieser Form möglich) zum Ausdruck gebracht.

    We should inform them immediately.
    Wir sollten sie sofort informieren.

    We ought to warn her.
    Wir sollten sie (eigentlich) warnen.

- *To be supposed to* drückt aus, was jemand tun soll, weil er durch Regeln, Vereinbarungen oder die Pflicht dazu angehalten ist. Die Formen existieren in Präsens und Imperfekt.

    A junior clerk is supposed to distribute letters.
    Von einem Bürogehilfen wird erwartet, daß er die Briefe verteilt.

    You are not supposed to use the firm's telephone for private calls.
    Man soll das Geschäftstelefon nicht für Privatgespräche benutzen.

Übung 13

Ändern Sie die vorliegenden Sätze so ab, daß in ihnen eine Form des Sollens (shall, should, to be supposed to, should have) vorkommt. Zu Ihrer Hilfe ist in Klammern der Sinn des Sollens auf deutsch vorgegeben.

BEISPIEL We tell her about our sales policy. (Sollen wir ihr . . . ?)
Shall we tell her about our sales policy?

1 We underestimate them. (Wir sollten sie nicht . . .)
2 I take part in the contest. (Soll ich . . . teilnehmen?)

3 We introduce more efficient methods of control. (Sollten wir ... ?)
4 Another order from Ponelka Ltd. And do I do all the paperwork again? (Und ich soll wieder ... ?)
5 They have come at four. (Sie hätten ... kommen sollen.)
6 The security guards check whether the lights are switched off. (... sollen prüfen, ob ...)
7 We have to pay far too many small amounts by cheque. We ask them to open an account for us. (Sollen wir sie bitten, ... ?)
8 We have more experienced staff for the new machines. (Wir sollten ... haben.)
9 I will meet him at the station. (Soll ich ihn ... ?)
10 Trade Unions support the striking workers. (... sollten ... unterstützen.)

Übung 14

Vervollständigen Sie die Sätze mit Formen des Sollens. Should ist die häufigste Form, die oft auch, vor allem umgangssprachlich, ought to und be supposed to verdrängt. Mehrere Antworten sind manchmal möglich.

1 We sent him the right pattern but the wrong sizes. What ... we do now?
2 You ... be at the ticket office an hour before the train leaves.
3 The airmail label ... not be forgotten.
4 ... we agree to their conditions?
5 We ... tell him the truth about the incident.
6 We ... not waste our energy trying to keep him with the company if he definitely wants to leave.
7 It's in the contract. We ... confirm the orders within three days.
8 She represents our company abroad. We ... give her more information about our production plans.
9 The goods are ruined. The exporter ... packed them in waterproof crates.
10 You ... always check in at least an hour before the plane takes off.

To be said to

♦ *To be said to* wird ebenfalls nur im Präsens und Imperfekt gebraucht und entspricht dem deutschen ‚Sollen' in der Wiedergabe eines Gerüchts oder einer Vermutung.

They are said to be prompt payers.
Sie sollen pünktliche Zahler sein.

Übung 15

Bei dieser Übung handelt es sich um Aussage- und Fragesätze in einem Gespräch. Die Lücken sind mit den englischen Entsprechungen von ‚sollen' (should, be supposed to, be said to) zu füllen. Es kann mehrere richtige Lösungen geben.

Penny and Lucy are in the administration manager's office when Tom comes into the room.

1 Tom   What are you doing here apart from looking out of the window? You . . . be tidying up the office for Mr James' first day with us tomorrow.
2 Penny   We . . . have everything ready by late afternoon, but we won't be able to if everybody keeps interrupting us.
3 Lucy   Tom, did you know that Mr James . . . have plans for completely restructuring our administrative system?
4 Tom   Yes, he . . . make our administrative system work more efficiently, whatever that means.
    Penny   Is there anybody who knows him already?
5 Tom   Bill . . . have worked with him a couple of years ago.
    Lucy   And what does he say about him?
6 Tom   We . . . be prepared for some changes.
    Lucy   I would like to know what type of man he is.
7 Tom   He . . . be short-tempered.
    Penny   Don't believe everything that is said about him.
8 Penny   Do you think he would like some flowers on his desk? . . . I get some?
9 Tom   I don't know, but I'm sure he won't like people who . . . be working standing around talking.

Wollen (to wish, to be willing to, to intend to, to mean to, to want)

♦ Mit dem Verb ‚wollen' können wir im Deutschen eine ganze Reihe von Willenshaltungen ausdrücken, und für jede von ihnen hat die englische Sprache entsprechende Ersatzformen.

  ◊ **Wunsch** – to wish
    I don't wish to disturb you.
    Ich will Sie nicht stören.

    They wish to replace the old model with a new one.
    Sie wollen das alte Modell durch ein neues ersetzen.

  ◊ **Bereitschaft** – to be willing to
    He is always willing to help.
    Er ist immer willens zu helfen.

  ◊ **Absicht** – to intend to, to mean to
    We never intended to keep it.
    Wir haben es nie behalten wollen.

    He did not mean to be rude.
    Er wollte nicht unhöflich sein.

  ◊ **Verlangen oder Bedürfnis** – to want
    All we want is a holiday.
    Alles, was wir wollen, ist Urlaub.

    He wants to be promoted.
    Er will befördert werden.

Übung 16

Vervollständigen Sie die Sätze mit Hilfe der in Klammern angegebenen Begriffen. Je nach Absicht des Sprechers wären in einigen Fällen mehrere Lösungen möglich. Um zu eindeutigen Aussagen zu kommen, ist die Sprecherabsicht in Klammern angegeben.

BEISPIEL   We . . . to lower our prices. (Bereitschaft)
   We are willing to lower our prices.

1   Do you really . . . to go there without asking him? (Absicht)
2   We . . . to settle the matter quickly. (Wunsch)
3   We . . . a reliable representative for the area. (Bedürfnis)
4   We . . . to open an account with them. (Verlangen)
5   As a rule we do not exchange money, but we . . . to help you in this case. (Bereitschaft)
6   We . . . to have the case settled by arbitration. (Absicht)
7   I . . . to withdraw some money from my account. (Verlangen)
8   He . . . to let me give his name as a referee. (Bereitschaft)
9   They . . . the goods to be replaced. (Verlangen)
10 They . . . to call a second meeting of the shareholders. (Absicht)
11 I . . . to have the new system in operation by the end of the year. (Wunsch)
12 We . . . to deal with that rather unusual complaint. (Bereitschaft)
13 If we . . . to remain competitive, we must have new ideas. (Verlangen)
14 He said that he . . . to retire when he was 55. (Wunsch)
15 I . . . (not) to contradict her, but I think she is wrong. (Absicht)
16 We . . . to review the salary structure in the firm. (Verlangen, Bedürfnis)
17 We . . . to write job descriptions for the new jobs. (Absicht)
18 He . . . to make the necessary changes as soon as possible. (Absicht)

Übung 17

Diese gemischte Übung umfaßt nahezu alles, was Sie in dieser Einheit kennengelernt haben. Manchmal sind mehrere Antworten möglich.

1   We . . . agree to their conditions. (sollten)
2   May I make payments from a current account with cheques? (kurze, positive Antwort)

3 Do you ... to travel first class? (wollen, Wunsch)
4 More complex insurance documents ... be prepared to cover credit risks. (müssen)
5 We need better packaging. Who will pay for that? I'm sorry, but you ... pay for that. (müssen, Fut. 1)
6 The holder of a current account ... issue cheques for more than he has in his account. (darf)
7 However, he ... exceed his overdraft facility. (darf nicht)
8 I ... stay long. (will nicht, Absicht)
9 Problems like that ... happen in a company like ours. (können nicht)
10 We were making so little money that we ... meet our running costs. (konnten nicht)
11 If the terms of credit are 30 days, you ... be late with your payments. (dürfen nicht)
12 It is an important order. We ... book freight passage in advance. (sollten)
13 If we ... to be more commercially competitive, we ... spend more on research and development. (wollen, müssen)
14 In a partnership each partner ... put in the same amount of money. (muß)
15 We ... take measures to enforce the safety regulations. (mußten)
16 Sales and public relations ... work closely together. (sollten)
17 ... we supply you with our own packing cases and then get a 5% discount? (könnten)
18 I am afraid I ... consult our sales manager first. (muß)
19 Scotland ... be a vital market for us. (könnte)
20 We ... despatch it without delay. (müssen)
21 He ... his desk to be placed near the window. (wollte, Verlangen)
22 They ... be here by the end of the week. (könnten)
23 If you went there on your own, you ... pay for accommodation. (müssen, Kond. 1)
24 We ... reduce our costs. (müssen, Fut. 1)
25 We ... meet a lot of important people at the fair. (könnten)
26 The goods ... be packed according to our instructions. (müssen)
27 The delegation ... to tell us about the new heating system. (wollte, Absicht)
28 We know the difficulties, we ... warn him. (sollten)

7 Das Gerundium

Einführung

- Das Gerundium hat im Deutschen keine Entsprechung. Im Englischen ist es eine Verbform, die durch Anhängen von *-ing* an das Verb gebildet wird.

- Das Gerundium ist ein Wesensmerkmal der englischen Sprache und kann die Ausdrucksweise klar und die Formulierung kurz machen.

  She considered leaving the company but then changed her mind.
  Mr Reade hates his secretary being late.

- Grammatisch gesehen ist das Gerundium eine Mischform.

  ◇ Es kann substantivische Eigenschaften aufweisen:
  Bargaining is part of every trade.

  ◇ Es kann aber auch verbale Züge zeigen:
  She began writing the letter.
  He objected to being disturbed again.
  They apologized for having arrived (for arriving) late this morning.

- Die vier Formen des Gerundiums, von denen die erste die häufigste ist, sind:

	Präsens	Perfekt
Aktiv	typing	having typed
Passiv	being typed	having been typed

Die Klärung der grammatischen Begriffe

- **Subjekt**
 Das Subjekt kann man mittels folgender Fragewörter bestimmen: wer oder was?
 Die Aushilfskraft verpackt die Kataloge.
 wer oder was? – *die Aushilfskraft*

- **Akkusativobjekt (direktes Objekt)**
 Das Objekt wird durch die Fragewörter ermittelt: wen oder was?
 Die Aushilfskraft verpackt die Kataloge.
 wen oder was? – *die Kataloge.*

- **Prädikative Ergänzung**
 Was nach einer Form des Verbs ‚sein' (z.b. ist, bist, war, ist gewesen) steht, ist prädikative Ergänzung und gibt Auskunft über das Subjekt.
 Mrs Jenkins ist Verkaufsleiterin.

- **Ergänzung nach Präpositionen**
 Was nach einer Präposition folgt, gleich ob Verb + Präposition, Substantiv + Präposition oder Adjektiv + Präpositon, wollen wir hier der Einfachheit halber ‚Ergänzung nach Präpositionen' nennen.
 Wir warten auf *weitere Aufträge.*
 Es ist der Grund für *meine Abreise.*
 Er ist stolz auf *die Auszeichnung.*

- **Adverbiale Bestimmung**
 Adverbiale Bestimmungen geben die näheren Umstände einer Handlung an.
 Er prüfte die Zahlungseingänge,
    ◇ *bevor er abreiste.* (wann? temporal)
    ◇ *ohne etwas zu sagen.* (wie? modal)
    ◇ *da er den Fehler finden wollte.* (warum? kausal)
    ◇ *indem er die Kontoauszüge prüfte.* (wie, wodurch? instrumental)
    ◇ *obwohl es schon spät war.* (Gegensatz zum Hauptsatz)

Das Gerundium als Subjekt

◆ Das Gerundium kann wie ein Substantiv als Subjekt eines Satzes benutzt werden.

Filing is one of his main duties.
Typing is something all secretaries have to do.
Having nice colleagues at work is important to Susan.

Übung 1

Verwandeln Sie die gegebenen Infinitive in Gerundien.

BEISPIEL   It is impolite to interrupt someone on the phone.
Interrupting someone on the phone is impolite.

1   It is interesting to listen to her.
2   It is stupid to try it again.
3   It is risky to start a new sales campaign at this time of the year.
4   It is too expensive to take out a loan with interest rates as high as 15%.
5   It is too dangerous to send these goods by ship.
6   It is embarrassing to admit a mistake.
7   It is stupid to disregard safety regulations.
8   It is rude to send a letter without a complimentary close.
9   It is sad to see the work-force reduced.
10 It is very annoying to have an instruction manual with too many cross-references in it.
11 It is not healthy to work in an office without any windows.
12 It used to be a slow job to operate a telex machine.
13 It is much easier to fax a letter.
14 It is wise to replace an employee who is lazy.
15 It is encouraging to see the sales increase after an advertising campaign.

Das Gerundium als logisches Subjekt

- Das Gerundium steht nach bestimmten Wendungen:

it is (not) worthwhile	es lohnt sich (nicht)
it is no use (good)	es hat keinen Zweck
it is not much use (good)	es hat nicht viel Zweck
It is no use asking them again.	

- In den folgenden Fällen können Sie das Gerundium oder den Infinitiv verwenden:

it is useless	es ist zwecklos
it is hard	es fällt schwer
it is a pleasure	es ist ein Vergnügen
it is fun	es macht Spaß
It is useless giving (to give) them advice.	

Übung 2

Bilden Sie das Gerundium oder den Infinitiv des <u>unterstrichenen</u> Satzteiles. Hinter der Aufgabe finden Sie jeweils einen Vorschlag, der Ihnen eine geeignete Wendung anbietet.

BEISPIELE   She is busy now. <u>Don't wait</u> for her. (It is no use . . .)
She is busy now. It is no use waiting for her.
<u>I cannot make</u> a statement on future sales. (It is hard . . .)
It is hard making (to make) a statement on future sales.

1. There is no money in the market. <u>Now is a bad time to set up</u> one's own firm. (It is not worthwhile . . .)
2. This time our competitors were faster than we were. <u>It will not pay to invest</u> more money in the project. (It is not worthwhile . . .)
3. <u>I like to watch</u> Penny. She knows how to get on with difficult customers. (It is a pleasure . . .)
4. They have declared the company bankrupt. <u>We should not send</u> them another request for payment. (It is not much use . . .)

5   The customer angrily left the shop and banged the door. It's too late to apologize now. (It is no use . . .)
6   His excuse sounded very strange. Can we accept it? (It is hard . . .)
7   He flatly refused to give us a payrise. We won't ask him again. (It is no use . . .)
8   She said she speculated on the Stock Exchange for the fun of it. (She said it was fun . . .)
9   It is easy to get a loan. To repay one's debt on time is just the opposite. (It is hard . . .)
10 We work in a very damp room without ventilation. It is not easy. (It is hard . . .)
11 If we overcome this difficulty, we will have won. It will pay if we work hard now. (It's worthwhile . . .)
12 She has been made redundant. But it does not help to feel disappointed and angry. (It's no use . . .)

Das Gerundium als direktes Objekt

♦   Das Gerundium kann als direktes Objekt stehen.

Tom enjoys having lunch with Penny.
Tom freut sich, mit Penny zu Mittag zu essen.

Barbara hates filing.
Barbara haßt es, die Ablage zu machen.

♦   Es gibt bestimmte Verben, nach denen das Gerundium stehen muß, andere, nach denen das Gerundium (oder der Infinitiv) stehen kann, und eine dritte Gruppe, in der das Gerundium und der Infinitiv verschiedene Aussagen bewirken.

◇ Das Gerundium steht nach folgenden Verben:

to admit	zugeben
to appreciate	schätzen
to avoid	vermeiden
to consider	erwägen
to deny	leugnen
to dislike	nicht gern tun (mögen)
to enjoy	Freude haben an
to escape	entkommen
to excuse	entschuldigen
to finish	beenden
to give up	aufgeben
to go (keep) on	fortfahren, weitermachen
to imagine	sich vorstellen
to include	einschließen
to justify	rechtfertigen
to mind	etwas dagegen haben
to miss	vermeiden, verpassen
to practise	üben
to reject	zurückweisen
to risk	wagen
to stop	aufhören mit
I cannot help	ich kann nicht umhin

◇ Nach folgenden Verben steht das Gerundium oder der Infinitiv:

to allow	erlauben
to attempt	versuchen
to begin	anfangen mit (zu)
to cease	aufhören mit
to continue	fortfahren mit
to hate	hassen, nicht mögen
to intend	beabsichtigen
to like	mögen
to love	lieben
to prefer	bevorziehen
to start	anfangen mit (zu)

Übung 3

Vervollständigen Sie die Sätze und bilden Sie das Gerundium mit dem unterstrichenen Verb.

BEISPIEL   She is an excellent typist and <u>types</u> without any mistakes. And she really enjoys . . .
And she really enjoys typing.

1 We have always <u>sent</u> invoices on the day of despatch. We will keep on . . .
2 She <u>writes</u> covering letters that are attached to our invoices. She is practising . . .
3 They did not answer any of our reminders. We plan to <u>take</u> legal action now. We are considering . . .
4 It is their fourth large order in three months. I think we shall <u>offer</u> them credit in the form of an open account. I think we can justify . . .
5 Since the introduction of computers we do not <u>send</u> advice notes and acknowledgements of payments any longer. Since the introduction of computers we have given up . . .
6 We have not had any orders from them for a long time. We cannot <u>grant</u> them the 10% special discount any longer. We must stop . . .
7 We have not received payment from our customers because of the strike. We will also <u>be</u> less punctual in settling our accounts. We cannot avoid . . .
8 Although they have not settled their account, we do not want to <u>lose</u> them as one of our best customers. We cannot risk . . .
9 If you have to explain why you cannot pay on time, don't <u>be</u> overdramatic. Avoid . . .
10 Mrs Jenkins' decision was to <u>wait</u> another week before sending them a third reminder. Mrs Jenkins said, "I don't mind . . ."

Das Gerundium als prädikative Ergänzung

- Das Gerundium kann nach Formen von *to be* und nach *to be busy* benutzt werden.

    His hobby is bargain hunting.
    Sein Hobby ist, nach Billigangeboten zu jagen.

    He is busy sorting the mail.
    Er ist damit beschäftigt, die Post zu sortieren.

Übung 4

Vervollständigen Sie die Sätze und verwenden Sie dabei das Gerundium.

BEISPIEL   (to distribute) His job is . . . the interdepartmental mail.
His job is distributing the interdepartmental mail.

1 (to file) One of the most important tasks in a busy office is . . .
2 (to get) His only ambition is . . . to the top of the company.
3 (to study) He is busy . . . the results of the quality control report.
4 (to be made redundant) I have a wife and four children and my concern is . . . .
5 (to be an expert) He is the right man for the complaints section. His advantage is . . . in handling difficult customers.
6 (to work on the draft contract) I am afraid she has no time now. She is busy . . .
7 (to be not flexible) She is an excellent chairperson. But one of her faults is . . .
8 (to be selected) The one thing that pleased her most last year was . . . for the senior management course in Edinburgh.
9 (to be involved) It was too much for him. His main problem was . . . in too many arguments.
10 (to be too sensitive) It's true that he made a small mistake and he knows it. But he needn't worry. His weakness is . . .

Das Gerundium als präpositionale Ergänzung

- Das Gerundium kann nach Präpositionen in Verbindung mit einem Verb, einem Substantiv und einem Adjektiv stehen. Der entscheidende Satzteil ist unterstrichen.

  ◊ **Verb + Präposition**
  He <u>is thinking of</u> giving up his job.
  Er denkt daran, seine Arbeit aufzugeben.

to agree to/with	zustimmen
to apologize for	sich entschuldigen für
to ask about	fragen nach
to begin by	anfangen mit
to believe in	glauben an
to complain about	sich beklagen über
to concentrate on	sich konzentrieren auf
to consist of	bestehen aus
to cope with	fertigwerden mit
to decide against	sich entscheiden gegen
to depend on	sich verlassen auf
to look forward to	sich freuen auf
to object to	widersprechen
to pay for	bezahlen für
to prevent from	hindern an
to rely on	sich verlassen auf
to spend on	ausgeben für
to succeed in	Erfolg haben bei
to take part in	teilnehmen an
to talk about	sprechen über
to think of	denken an
to thank for	danken für
to worry about	sich beunruhigen wegen

◇ **Substantiv + Präposition**
We have no objection to using the new machines.
Wir haben nichts dagegen, die neuen Maschinen zu benutzen.

to take advantage of	Vorteil ziehen aus
to have a choice between	die Wahl haben zwischen
to be in danger of	in Gefahr sein zu
to have no doubt about	keinen Zweifel daran haben zu
to have some experience in	Erfahrung haben in
to have an interest in	ein Interesse haben an
to have no objection to	keinen Einwand dagegen haben zu
to have the pleasure of	das Vergnügen haben
to take pleasure in	Spaß haben an
to be on the point of	im Begriff sein zu
to consider the possibility of	die Möglichkeit erwägen zu
to have a problem in	Schwierigkeiten haben mit
to have a reason for	einen Grund haben zu

◇ **Adjektiv + Präposition**
Mr Reade is tired of saying it again and again.
Mr Reade hat es satt, es immer wieder zu sagen.

capable of	fähig zu
clever at	gut in
delighted about	entzückt über
disappointed about/at	enttäuscht über
enthusiastic about	begeistert von
excited about	aufgeregt über
far from	weit entfernt von
free from	frei von
impressed with	beeindruckt von
incapable of	unfähig zu
interested in	interessiert an
keen on	sehr interessiert an
responsible for	verantwortlich für
tired of	genug haben von

- Hier sind noch weitere Ausdrücke, nach denen das Gerundium steht. Einige werden wie präpositionale Wendungen benutzt:

Tom does not feel like working.
Tom ist nicht nach Arbeit zumute.

How about starting again?
Wie wär's, wenn wir nochmals von vorn anfingen?

What about rewriting the whole letter?
Wie wär's, wenn wir den ganzen Brief neu schrieben?

Übung 5

Beantworten Sie die Fragen, indem Sie die Vorgaben benutzen und das Gerundium verwenden.

BEISPIEL   What are safety officers responsible for? (take all necessary steps to avoid accidents)
They are responsible for taking all necessary steps to avoid accidents.

1. What is a thief accused of? (steal)
2. What does a sales representative concentrate on? (get orders)
3. What are they famous for? (produce only high quality furniture)
4. What did our marketing department spend all the money on? (advertise the new model)
5. What do sales people dream of? (get higher commissions)
6. What does the shop-steward object to? (work longer hours)
7. What does the new operator have experience in? (handle computers)
8. Negotiations have become tough. What is our sales manager far from? (give up)
9. What is the sales manager's assistant engaged in? (prepare a sales exhibition)
10. They already get the 20 plus 8 per cent we allow our best customers. What are we incapable of? (grant them a higher discount)
11. Our MD is in Tokyo at the moment. The city's street signs are written in Japanese. What does he have trouble in? (find his way)
12. She is studying our competitor's catalogue. What is she very clever at? (find the weak points in their range of products)

Übung 6

Ordnen Sie unter Verwendung des Gerundiums die Satzhälften einander zu.

1. We are in danger of
2. The three companies have just succeeded in
3. She is far from
4. We have a good chance of
5. We are keen on
6. Our sales manager is delighted about
7. She is enthusiastic about
8. Personnel say that there is a possibility of
9. We look forward to
10. Unfortunately he is incapable of

a receive further orders from you
b work in a big company like ours
c merge with yet another company
d be pushed out of the market
e get that big order from the USA
f beat them on their home market
g win the contract if we keep cool
h admit he has made a mistake
i go to England on a management course but nothing is certain yet
j give up her plans

Übung 7

Setzen Sie in dieser Übung sowohl ein Gerundium als auch eine Präposition (durch drei Pünktchen (. . .) angedeutet) ein.

BEISPIEL They are thinking . . . (sell) new shares by advertising.
They are thinking of selling new shares by advertising.

1. Are you insisting . . . (have) a monthly report?
2. I am afraid . . . (be) nervous at the interview.
3. He is responsible . . . (check) incoming goods.
4. They are a very small firm, but I look forward . . . (cooperate) with them.
5. Fortunately she has given . . . (complain) about the canteen food.
6. You will have an opportunity . . . (meet) the production manager, too.
7. A "Business Reply Service" gives customers the chance . . . (write) to firms without paying any postage.
8. Is he happy . . . (move) to a new department.
9. She is looking forward . . . (meet) her new boss.
10. He's worried . . . (lose) the contract.

Das Gerundium als adverbiale Bestimmung (Umstandsbestimmung)

- Adverbiale Bestimmungen geben die näheren Umstände einer Handlung an. Es gibt adverbiale Bestimmungen

  - **der Zeit** (after, before, on, since, when)
    We must complete the order before going to France.
    Wir müssen den Auftrag fertig machen, bevor wir nach Frankreich gehen.

  - **der Art u. Weise** (without, with, in, instead of)
    He left his office without leaving a message for you.
    Er verließ sein Büro, ohne etwas für Sie zu hinterlassen.

  - **des Grundes** (for, from, at)
    She got red eyes from working too long at the computer.
    Sie bekam entzündete Augen, weil sie zu lange an ihrem Computer arbeitete.

  - **des Mittels** (by, in, in doing so)
    She passed her typing test by putting in many hours of practice.
    Sie bestand ihren Schreibmaschinentest, weil sie viele Übungsstunden investiert hatte.

  - **der Einräumung** (in spite of)
    In spite of making those concessions, we will make a nice profit on this contract.
    Obwohl wir diese Konzessionen gemacht haben, werden wir mit diesem Vertrag einen guten Profit erzielen.

Übung 8

Verbinden Sie beide Sätze mit Hilfe der Wörter in Klammern.

BEISPIEL   We left the trade fair. We did not place an order. (without)
We left the trade fair without placing an order.

1 They went to the Information Point. They landed at Heathrow. (after)
2 We got the order. We made the best offer. (by)

3 He put down the receiver. He did not apologize. (without)
4 She has not reached the sales target. She got her own area. (since)
5 They profited from our generous discount scheme. They agreed to our usual terms of payment. (by)
6 He was removed from the team. He was absent from work more often than he needed to be. (for)
7 You have to finish all your sales calls. Then you chase up bad debts. (before)
8 She got very angry. She heard about the number of unpaid customer accounts. (on)
9 They delivered all the parcels. They were completely exhausted. (in spite of)
10 He has become very popular with the staff. He always offers help if anybody has a problem. (by)

Übung 9

Wandeln Sie einen der beiden gegebenen Satzteile mit Hilfe der in Klammern angegebenen Wörter in ein Gerundium um.

BEISPIEL   When we had compared prices we placed a trial order. (after)
After comparing prices, we placed a trial order.

1 Before you buy something on hire purchase, you should find out the selling price. (before)
2 After you have learnt the selling price, ask what the deposit is. (after)
3 You know the rate of interest, but you might be surprised by the number and size of the instalments. (in spite of)
4 If you haven't got all the details, you cannot find out whether hire purchase is to your advantage. (without)
5 A worker knows the hours he or she has worked because he or she will use a clock card. (by)
6 A wages clerk takes the times stamped on the card and thus he can calculate the total hours worked each day. (by)
7 He subtracts the normal daily working hours from the hours actually worked and in this way gets the hours of overtime. (by)
8 They had found that they actually needed more money than they had, they asked their bank for a loan. (after)

Das Gerundium mit eigenem Subjekt

- Wenn Sie einen Satz im Gerundium sehen, ist im Normalfall das Subjekt des Hauptsatzes auch Träger der Handlung, die im Gerundium ausgedrückt wird.
  In diesem Beispielsatz ist *We* das Subjekt, und beide Verben, *look forward* und *hearing* beziehen sich darauf:
  We look forward to hearing from you soon.

- Das Gerundium kann aber ein eigenes Subjekt haben:
  Mr Reade insisted on Henry (or him) leaving immediately.
  Mr Reade bestand darauf, daß Henry (oder er) sofort abfuhr.

Übung 10

Verkürzen Sie diese Sätze, indem Sie Gerundien verwenden. In einigen Fällen müssen Sie eine passende Präposition finden.

BEISPIEL   Our MD cannot understand that Mrs Jenkins is urging him to take on more sales staff.
Our MD cannot understand Mrs Jenkins urging him to take on more staff.

1 She does not mind if the girls smoke, but the stock room is a no-smoking area.
2 Do you remember that this man applied for the same job a year ago?
3 I cannot understand that our attorney did not answer our letter.
4 The team strongly dislikes the fact that the foreman will be transferred.
5 He dislikes it if our customers ask for last minute appointments.
6 They were afraid that the Trade Minister would raise import quotas.
7 We objected that the personnel manager gave away three of our office rooms.
8 Nobody likes the idea that Miss Wood is leaving the company.
9 We dislike it if our supplier makes excuses for the delay.
10 We do not mind if our night watchmen have their dogs with them.
11 I'm afraid that the main speaker will be late again.
12 She hates it if her trainees are late.

Übung 11

Bilden Sie in dieser gemischten Übung aus zwei Sätzen unter Verwendung des Gerundiums einen Satz.

BEISPIEL   He wants to check the incomplete consignment himself. He insists on it.
He insists on checking the incomplete consignment himself.

1 She is not negligent. You cannot accuse her of that.
2 You will get the components in time. You can depend on it.
3 The new salesman has got a bonus. He is very proud of it.
4 She works in a big company. She is proud of it.
5 She asked you to bring the confidential letters. Do you remember?
6 I don't mind. They can sell the old machines in new boxes.
7 Mr Reade visits our subsidiaries unexpectedly. He is fond of doing so.
8 She laughed at his tricks. She could not help it.
9 They had exceeded the sales target. They got a prize for it.
10 She has been removed from the shortlist. I object.

8 Das Partizip

Einführung

- Partizipien sind Formen des Verbs, die in der Regel durch Anfügen von *-ing* oder *-ed* gebildet werden und die sowohl adjektivische *(an exciting trip)* als auch verbale *(I saw him crossing the hall)* Eigenschaften haben können.

- Wie das Gerundium wird im englischen Satzbau das Partizip verwendet, um eine Aussage kurz und präzise zu machen. Im Deutschen braucht man häufig wesentlich umfangreichere Satzgebilde, um einen Partizipialsatz zu übersetzen.

  Having his own area he could increase his monthly sales figures.
  Da er seinen eigenen Bezirk hatte, konnte er seine monatlichen Verkaufszahlen erhöhen.

- Die Formen des Partizips

	Präsens	**Perfekt**
Aktiv	*working* *being* *having*	*(having) worked* *(having) been* *(having) had*
Passiv	*being seen*	*having been seen*

Das Partizip als Ergänzung zum Subjekt

- Das Partizip macht eine zusätzliche Aussage zum Subjekt, und zwar nach den Verben der Ruhe (*to sit, to stand, to lie* usw.) und der Bewegung (*to go, to run, to walk, to come, to leave* usw.)

  He stood watching the workers at their machines.
  Er stand da und beobachtete die Arbeiter an ihren Maschinen.

  He left the room smiling.
  Er verließ lächelnd das Zimmer.

Übung 1

Suchen Sie aus den Verben in Klammern die passenden aus und setzen Sie sie in der richtigen (Partizipial-) Form in die Lücken ein.

BEISPIEL She walked in ... (cry, smile, sleep) and told us that she had passed the test.
She walked in smiling and told us that she had passed the test.

The production manager arrived in the canteen to find a group of employees deep in discussion. They asked him to join them and he did so ... (smile, shout, run)[1]. Most of the group sat there ... (sing, smoke, stand)[2], while a few of them stood at the window ... (drink, sniff, eat)[3] cups of tea and ... (drink, smoke, eat)[4] chocolate biscuits. They were talking about the low morale and general lack of commitment shown by two of the new trainees in the firm. The foreman said that he had been very angry on arriving at work that morning. John had been lying on a pile of packing material, ... (sleep, dance, scream)[5] soundly. When disturbed, he had got up ... (think, protest, smile)[6] that he had merely been testing the strength of the material. The foreman also said that John took much longer for lunch than he was supposed to and often returned ... (scream, grumble, whisper)[7] that the hours he had to work were far too long.

The production manager also heard from one of the supervisors about the new junior clerk, Alison. The supervisor said that every day that week, Alison had come ... (complain, contact, insist)[8] to her about one small thing or another. The day before the supervisor had stood ... (hear, listen, say)[9] to her talking about how dull the office was for a whole half an hour.

Das Partizip als Ergänzung zum direkten Objekt

♦ Das Partizip macht eine zusätzliche Aussage zum Objekt nach Verben der sinnlichen Wahrnehmung (to see, to hear, to feel, to notice, to watch, to observe, to listen to usw.). Allerdings kann in diesen Fällen sowohl das Partizip als auch der Infinitiv stehen.
Sie entscheiden sich für das Partizip wenn Sie im einfachen Satz die Verlaufsform nehmen würden (Vorgänge von einiger Dauer, Handlungen, die gerade stattfinden).
Der Infinitiv wird verwendet, wenn Sie im normalen Satz die einfache Zeitform wählen würden (kurze oder schnell aufeinanderfolgende Handlungen oder Vorgänge, deren Dauer unwesentlich ist).

BEISPIELE
He heard the workers discussing the new regulations.
Er hörte, wie die Arbeiter die neuen Bestimmungen diskutierten.

She saw the man jump down from the assembly line.
Sie sah den Mann vom Montageband herunterspringen.

Übung 2

Setzen Sie die Verben entweder in der Form des Partizips oder des Infinitivs in die Lücken ein. Es gibt gelegentlich zwei richtige Lösungen.

BEISPIELE You can see her ... (work) at her desk.
You can see her working at her desk.
I saw the forklift ... (hit) the gate.
I saw the forklift hit the gate.

1 I once heard her ... (give) a speech to the new staff.
2 We saw John ... (take) his clock card and then we left, too.
3 Let's observe him ... (repair) the machine.
4 During lunch break you can see them ... (play) cards.
5 She noticed him ... (unplug) the machine.
6 She has been given the instructions. When I came in yesterday I saw her ... (read) the leaflet.
7 I heard her ... (bang) the door when she left.
8 I heard the foreman ... (warn) him not to be late again.

9   They had their differences. I saw them ... (argue) about the terms.
10 I saw the shredder ... (be) plugged into the electricity supply.
11 We were discussing the problem when we heard her ... (knock) at the door.
12 The Safety Officer listened attentively to her ... (report) the accident.
13 Before she fell down we watched her ... (put) the files on the highest shelf.
14 Listen! I can hear the taxi ... (come).
15 This morning he was in a bad temper. I saw him ... (enter), ... (pass) the reception desk, ... (go) up the stairs, ... (rush) in to his room and ... (sit) down at his desk immediately.

Übung 3

Finden Sie selbst zu den Sätzen sinnvolle Ergänzungen. Benutzen Sie Verben der sinnlichen Wahrnehmung und entscheiden Sie zwischen Infinitiv und Partizip. Es gibt gelegentlich zwei richtige Lösungen.

BEISPIEL   The meeting is over now. I can ... them ... (come out).
The meeting is over now. I can hear them coming out.

1   I was in Mrs Jenkins' office this morning and ... her ... (talk) on the phone to them.
2   There can be no doubt about the machine any longer. We ... it ... (work perfectly).
3   Has she succeeded? – I think so, Tom. I ... her ... (leave smiling).
4   She must have been shocked. I ... her ... (turn pale).
5   He had ordered far too much stationery. We ... him ... (be) blamed for it.
6   The contract has been won. I ... her ... (sign it).
7   They are not working now. I can ... them ... (talk).
8   Is the water boiling over? I can ... something ... (bubble).
9   It was Jack who broke the pressure gauge. I ... him ... (drop it).
10 I ... it ... (fall and break).
11 Tom reacted very quickly. I ... him ... (grab) the fire extinguisher and ... (put out) the fire.
12 We have run out of recycled paper. I ... Susan ... (order) some more on the phone today.

Lassen (to leave, to keep) und Veranlassen

- Das Partizip steht nach den Verben des Lassens *(to leave, to keep)*.

  We left the problem unsolved.
  Wir ließen das Problem ungelöst.

  They kept me waiting for one hour.
  Sie ließen mich eine Stunde warten.

- Das Partizip steht nach *have* und *get* in der Bedeutung des Veranlassens:
  to have something done, to get something done: etwas machen lassen; veranlassen, daß etwas getan wird.

  They had (are having) the reception area painted.
  Sie ließen (lassen) den Empfangsbereich streichen.

Übung 4

Setzen Sie die Partizipien der in Klammern angegebenen Verben in die Lücken ein, und beachten Sie die verschiedenen Arten von Partizipien.

BEISPIELE Why does Tom always leave his things ... (lie) about?
Why does Tom always leave his things lying about?
The doors of the stock room should always be kept ... (lock).
The doors of the stock room should always be kept locked.

1 They kept us ... (wait) for an answer.
2 They have the containers ... (seal) to protect them from sea water.
3 We have the out-dated equipment ... (replace) every five years.
4 We left the containers ... (stand) in the yard untouched, as per instructions of the insurance agent.
5 When did you have the photocopiers ... (service)?
6 We have our wordprocessors ... (check) once a year.
7 We kept her ... (work) on the tender until yesterday.
8 I had the cylinders ... (exchange) two weeks ago.

Übung 5

Setzen Sie die Verben des Lassens oder Veranlassens (have, keep, leave) in die Lücken ein.

BEISPIEL We should ... one of the foremen replaced.
We should have one of the foremen replaced.

1 We should ... the pressure checked.
2 He ... the 1993 files stored in the old filing cabinet.
3 We will ... the matter put right immediately.
4 I ... her waiting for the clients in the reception area.
5 We ... the goods distributed to our outlets before the season began.
6 They ... me establishing contacts with new suppliers, a job I really like doing.
7 They ... processing the same data over and over again.
8 We ... this order cancelled because the buyer was clearly unable to pay.
9 We ... the containers locked in the storeroom until the delivery date.
10 We ... the portable computers equipped with our own software.

Übung 6

Setzen Sie die richtige Form des Partizips in die Lücken ein.

BEISPIEL We had our catalogue ... (update) by a professional agency.
We had our catalogue updated by a professional agency.

1 We had all the leaflets ... (distribute) before the season began.
2 We have the containers ... (label) for shipment to Brazil.
3 They had their commissions ... (cut) and they protested.
4 We have her ... (look) into the matter.
5 I spent a lot of money on fares. I must have my expenses ... (reimburse).
6 Where are they now? We left them ... (sort) out the faulty items in the yard.
7 She was kept ... (wait) for some time.
8 Our heating system is out-dated. We should have it ... (replace) before next winter.

Das Partizip in der Funktion eines Relativsatzes

- Das Partizip kann in der Funktion eines Relativsatzes stehen.
  (Frage: was für ein, welcher?)
  Diese Konstruktion wirkt meistens satzverkürzend.

The man speaking to the workers was the personnel manager.
(The man who was speaking to . . .)
Der Mann, der zu den Arbeitern sprach, war der Personalchef.

The instruction manual given to us proved to be most useful.
(The instruction manual which had been given to . . .)
Das Handbuch, das man uns gegeben hatte, erwies sich als äußerst nützlich.

Übung 7

Verkürzen Sie die folgenden Sätze, indem Sie Partizipialkonstruktionen verwenden. Es können Partizipien der Gegenwart (z.B. writing) oder der Vergangenheit (z.B. written) auftreten.

BEISPIELE A company that does not have marketing expertise will soon see its profits shrink.
A company not having marketing expertise will soon see its profits shrink.
An executive who is sent out to run an unprofitable subsidiary abroad faces a difficult task.
An executive sent out to run an unprofitable subsidiary abroad faces a difficult task.

1 The management meeting that is taking place this afternoon will be chaired by Mr Reade.
2 The suggestions that were made at the meeting will be discussed at a later date.
3 The advertisement that was published in the national newspapers resulted in more than two hundred applications.
4 A company that does not offer sufficient opportunities for staff training may well experience a high turnover of staff.

5 A company that shows a caring attitude towards its staff is likely to succeed.
6 Candidates who apply for higher management positions must be assessed by the personnel department.
7 A company that does not have a fair promotion system will also have discontented staff.
8 The assessment department that we established two years ago has proved to be an excellent asset.
9 Executives who criticize our assessment department have been told that assessment of all staff is company policy.
10 A group of countries that has no internal tariff barriers is called a single market.
11 Decisions in the EU are taken by the Council of Ministers which is made up of government ministers from each of the member states.
12 Representatives who sit in the European Parliament are called MEPs (Members of the European Parliament).
13 The body that runs the day-to-day business of the Community is the European Commission.
14 The European Court is the institution that deals with governments or companies who do not abide by the rules.

Das Partizip als verkürzter Adverbialsatz

◆ Sie können Nebensätze, die mit den Konjunktionen *when, after, although, if, as* und *since* beginnen, durch Partizipialkonstruktionen verkürzen.

When she opened the door, she saw the customer standing at the reception desk.
Opening the door, she saw the customer standing at the reception desk.

After she had welcomed her, she asked her to come to her office.
Having welcomed her, she asked her to come to her office.

Übung 8

Ersetzen Sie den am Anfang stehenden Nebensatz durch eine Partizipialfügung. Zwei Partizipialformen sind möglich, z.B. working und having worked.

BEISPIEL   When Mrs Jenkins saw how terrible the weather was, she called a taxi.
Seeing how terrible the weather was Mrs Jenkins called a taxi.

1. When Mr Reade came into his office next morning, he found the contract ready for signature.
2. As they both felt hungry, they went to the canteen to have a snack.
3. As they had worked hard all day, they felt rather tired.
4. When she had finished the letter, she had a cup of tea.
5. As she felt ill, she could not go to the interview.
6. As Penny had never worked for a big company before, she felt a little lost in the beginning.
7. As he did not want to admit his mistake, he paid the sum from his salary.
8. As he had lost the requisition form, he had to fill in another one.
9. As we were refused an import licence, we had to cancel the order.
10. When they had discussed prices again, they were able to come to an agreement.
11. As she had forgotten the departure time, she was at the check-in far too early.
12. As they did not quite understand some of the terms, they had to call the insurance company again.
13. Since she had worked on the development of the new system, she was asked to write a report.
14. Since we have carried out a survey of our employees' attitudes to their jobs, we can draw conclusions about necessary changes.
15. As she had not been promoted last year, she did not work as enthusiastically as before.

Übung 9

Bilden Sie Partizipialsätze und achten Sie auf die richtige Form des Partizips, z.B. calling , having called oder called.

BEISPIELE Richard saw an accident. He was more careful than before.
Having seen an accident, Richard was more careful than before.
We were disappointed with the quality of the paper. We complained to the supplier.
Disappointed with the quality of the paper, we complained to the supplier.

1 She passed the examination. She applied for a job advertised in a trade journal.
2 He exchanged the blades of the shredder. He got a bad cut.
3 He put out his cigarette. He entered the board room.
4 The apprentices had managed to do it alone. They proudly showed the machine to the foreman.
5 Sam read the job advertisements eagerly. He hoped for a stroke of luck.
6 They found the reason for the breakdown. They repaired the machine immediately.
7 She had worked for a similar company before. She overcame her initial difficulties in no time.
8 The machine was installed and connected last month. It has worked without any problems so far.
9 They were both sacked. They joined the unemployed.
10 He tripped over the carpet and dropped the dictating machine.
11 He hoped to go before the selection board. He improved his performance considerably.
12 Our suppliers were accused of not meeting the deadline. They had to pay a penalty.

Partizipialsätze mit einleitenden Konjunktionen

- Partizipialsätze können oft sehr verschieden verstanden werden.
  Properly trained, she is just the person for the job.
  (z.B.: da sie . . . , wenn sie . . . , nachdem sie . . .)

- Um Mißverständnisse zu vermeiden, werden oft Konjunktionen zur Einleitung der Partizipialsätze verwendet: *if, unless, whether, although, since, as, by, till, until, whenever.*

  If properly trained, she is . . .
  When properly trained, she is . . .
  Unless properly trained, she is . . .

Übung 10

Vervollständigen Sie die Sätze mit der passenden Konjunktion in den Klammern.

BEISPIEL   . . . having increased his sales, Jo still sold less than Jane.
(although, by, unless)
Although having increased his sales, Jo still sold less than Jane.

1. Don't call them back . . . told to do so. (unless, by, although)
2. . . . increasing commissions they hoped to improve their agents' performance. (by, if, although)
3. . . . reducing their range of products, the company is still financially healthy. (although, unless, until)
4. . . . filed properly all letters can be found easily. (until, while, if)
5. . . . confirmed by the seller an order remains an "offer to buy" and is not legally binding. (until, though, if)
6. . . . told to leave tomorrow I would object. (if, by, unless)
7. . . . having good relations with the workforce, he did not hear anything about the planned sit-in. (while, although, by)
8. We shall carry on . . . forced by the MD to give up. (if, while, unless)
9. Penny heard the argument . . . working at the copier. (while, until, by)
10. . . . lowering our prices we hope to be more competitive in that country. (if, by, while)

Partizipialkonstruktionen mit eigenem Subjekt

◆ Ähnlich wie das Gerundium (siehe Seite 122) kann auch eine Partizipialfügung ein eigenes Subjekt haben. Solche Partizipialfügungen, meist mit *with* eingeleitet, sind sehr gebräuchlich.

With the new range of products launched the company's market share became bigger.
With so many staff being off sick we can hardly keep pace with all the incoming orders.

Übung 11

Verbinden Sie die Satzteile zu einem sinnvollen Satzgefüge, indem Sie eine Partizipialfügung mit eigenem Subjekt bilden.

BEISPIEL ... (construction workers – to make a lot of noise) working at the computer became impossible
With the construction workers making a lot of noise, working at the computer became impossible.

1 ... (the go-ahead – to be given by the Board) the company is certain to make huge profits
2 ... (a lot of pickets – to stand at the gate) it was difficult for those who wanted to work to enter the factory
3 ... (the short list – to be finished) we can start writing invitations for the interviews
4 ... (the number of car thefts – to rise sharply) it will be difficult to keep insurance premiums down
5 ... (company cars – to be taxed now) firms have to think of other forms of fringe benefits
6 ... (the blinds – to be removed) it will be hard to work at the window
7 ... (import taxes – to be raised) we shall have difficulty holding our position in the market
8 ... (many young people – to intend to be bankers) it is not easy at the moment to find a position as a trainee
9 ... (demand – to fall, and all our costs – to increase) we must make some quality reductions
10 ... (Rix Ltd – to start a new sales campaign) competition will be fierce

Übung 12

In dieser gemischten Übung verwenden Sie alle Ihnen bekannten Partizipialkonstruktionen.

1. His commission was raised considerably. Charles jumped for joy. (His commission . . .)
2. We could hear them. They argued in the Board Room. (We . . .)
3. He took into account all possible options. Then he decided to transfer him to our Peruvian subsidiary. (After . . .)
4. The old SX model is no longer draining our budget. We could launch an elaborate campaign for our new high pressure system. (With . . .)
5. No worker will be satisfied if he is not given a fair pay. (. . . unless . . .)
6. She was not willing to wait for an answer. She asked for his decision on the spot. (Not . . .)
7. But they wanted to finish drafting the contracts before they went home. (Before . . .)
8. You may be asked. Don't tell them anything. (If . . .)
9. As our salesman was indecisive he lost the contract. (By . . .)
10. The foreman who was overlooked when it came to promotion left the company.
11. They were thoroughly trained for their new job. Their probation period was over. (After . . .)
12. Their working capital is adapted to the company's needs. Their financial position seems to be healthy. (With . . .)
13. Since I joined this company, I have not taken a single day off.
14. He saw the receptionist. She was making a telephone call.
15. He was often criticized for being late. He always had an excuse.
16. They put the finishing touches to the new office building. They could hardly wait to move out of the old offices.
17. If we have time, we shall celebrate her promotion in the "Yellow Submarine". (Benutzen Sie das Verb permit.)
18. He saw Mr Reade who was driving his new Jaguar.
19. The Chairman expressed his opinion on the matter, before he had collected all the available information. (Before . . .)
20. He arrived at the conclusion that we must reduce our costs by 10% and then cancelled all the company's sporting activities.

Der Infinitiv 9

Einführung

- Der Infinitiv ist eine Form des Verbs, die im Englischen wie im Deutschen häufig vorkommt. Eine ganze Reihe von Anwendungsformen des englischen Infinitivs ist uns daher wohl vertraut. Sie sehen an den folgenden Beispielen, daß bestimmte Anwendungsformen des englischen Infinitivs dem des deutschen parallel laufen.

  BEISPIELE
  To go by train is very pleasant.
  Mit dem Zug zu fahren ist sehr angenehm.

  She managed to win a prize.
  Sie schaffte es, einen Preis zu gewinnen.

  He always seems to be busy.
  Er scheint immer beschäftigt zu sein.

  He came back to tell us the results.
  Er kam zurück, um uns die Ergebnisse mitzuteilen.

  She can operate a computer.
  Sie kann mit einem Computer arbeiten.

- Der Infinitiv wirkt wie das Gerundium und das Partizip stark satzverkürzend, was seine weite Verbreitung im Englischen erklärt.

- Wie im Deutschen gibt es im Englischen zwei Arten des Infinitivs:
  ◇ **Einen Infinitiv mit *to***
     I refuse *to come.*
     Ich weigere mich zu kommen.

  ◇ **Einen Infinitiv ohne *to***
     I can *come.*
     Ich kann kommen.

Der Infinitiv mit to

♦ Die Formen des Infinitivs mit *to*:

	Präsens	Perfekt
Aktiv	to copy	to have copied
Passiv	to be copied	to have been copied

We ought *to copy* the agenda.
We ought *to have copied* the agenda.

The agenda ought *to be copied*.
The agenda ought *to have been copied*.

Der Infinitiv mit to als Attribut

♦ **Der Infinitiv mit *to* nach Substantiven**
Die englischen Formulierungen sind oft kürzer als die deutschen:

The parts to be checked are in our quality control centre.
... die geprüft werden sollen,
She has enough *experience to be* a supervisor.
... genug Erfahrung, um eine ... zu werden.

♦ **Der Infinitiv mit *to* nach Adjektiven**

He was *disappointed to see* that the new brand failed to sell.
They are *unlikely to be made* redundant.
She can be *sure to be promoted*.

♦ **Der Infinitiv mit *to* nach superlativischen Wendungen, Ordnungszahlen und *only***

The next problem to arise was the lack of staff.
The best thing to do is to make a fresh start.
This is *just the thing to make* him happy.
It is *the only thing to give* him satisfaction.

Übung 1

Verbinden Sie die vorgegebenen Sätze. Setzen Sie too vor das Adjektiv (z.B. too hot to . . .) oder enough nach dem Adjektiv (z.B. cold enough to . . .). Enough steht meistens vor dem Substantiv (z.B. enough money to . . .).

BEISPIEL   The junior clerk was silly. He lost the keys of the filing cabinet.
The junior clerk was silly enough to lose the keys of the filing cabinet.

1   She was clever. She passed the letter to a senior clerk.
2   Mrs Jenkins was angry. She could not talk to him.
3   Our chief buyer is sensible. He did not accept the offer.
4   We are busy. We can't have our usual tea break.
5   The box is bulky. It cannot be sent by post.
6   He was excited. He could not answer the questions.
7   At last he said he had a lot of money. He could buy our company.
8   The profit was not big. It did not get us out of our financial mess.
9   The lorry was not big. It could not take the whole consignment.
10 Penny is not tall. She cannot reach the top shelf.

Übung 2

Verkürzen Sie die Relativsätze durch die Verwendung von Infinitiv-Konstruktionen.

BEISPIELE   The next speaker who addressed the shareholders was the financial director.
The next speaker to address the shareholders was the financial director.
It is the last box that we dispatch today.
It is the last box to be dispatched today.

1   Bill was the last who left the meeting.
2   There was not a single person who could help them with the CAD programme.
3   When stopped at the gate he had nothing he could use as an excuse.
4   Our department was the first that had finished stocktaking.

5 She would have been the first who admits a mistake.
6 Only Tom did not see anything he could laugh about.
7 It was the worst thing that could happen to us.
8 Their order is the next that will be completed.
9 Helen was the first woman who became head of department.
10 The *Financial Times* is the best paper you can read if you are interested in business affairs.

Der Infinitiv mit to nach how, what, when, who, which, whether

◆ Der Infinitiv mit *to* nach dem Fragewörtern *how, what, when, who, which, whether* wird verwendet, um Sätze zu verkürzen.

He does not yet know where he should stay.
He does not yet know where to stay.

She knows very well how she should deal with difficult customers.
She knows very well how to deal with difficult customers.

Übung 3

Verkürzen Sie die folgenden Sätze, indem Sie einen Infinitiv nach dem Fragewort verwenden.

BEISPIEL   I don't know where I can find Mr Reade at the moment.
I don't know where to find Mr Reade at the moment.

1 She wondered what she should say after she was sacked.
2 Tom had better learn when he has to wear a tie.
3 Do you know how I can get to the receiving department?
4 Mr Reade did not know whether he should smile or be angry.
5 We do not yet know who we will invite for interview.
6 She knows very well how complaints can be settled.

7 We did not know what we should do with the goods which were below standard.
8 After this major problem I do not know whether we should maintain the business relationship or not.
9 He did not know where he could ask for further information.
10 They were not sure whether they should submit a counter offer.

Verb + Objekt + Infinitiv mit to

♦ Die Fügung *want/would like* + Objekt + Infinitiv drückt aus, daß das Subjekt des Satzes einen Wunsch in bezug auf das Objekt hat.

I want her to rearrange my flight to Munich.

♦ Diese Anwendung des Infinitivs ist auch möglich nach einer Reihe von Verben des Veranlassens, wie *to expect, to advise, to ask, to beg, to cause, to command, to force, to get, to order, to tell* (befehlen), *to urge* usw.

Mr Reade wants Mrs Jenkins to prepare the new offer today.
Mrs Jenkins would like Susan to make arrangements for the business trip immediately.

♦ Die gleiche Konstruktion ist auch möglich nach Verben des (Nicht) Wünschens und (Nicht) Wollens wie *to (dis)like, to hate, to prefer, to invite, to love, to warn* usw.

He warned him not to do it again.
She preferred them to park their cars outside the factory yard.

Merke: Nach *to say, to answer, to reply, to hope* und *to tell* (erzählen, sagen) ist nur die Konstruktion mit *that* möglich.

We hoped (that) they would deliver the goods the same day.
She said (that) she needed a new secretary as soon as possible.

Übung 4

Schreiben Sie die folgenden Sätze um, indem Sie beginnen wie in den Klammern angegeben.

BEISPIEL   They must open the boxes and check the contents. (I want . . .)
I want them to open the boxes and check the contents.

1 You must not interrupt Mr Reade. (I don't want . . .)
2 She must photocopy the contracts at once. (I expect . . .)
3 They should only send us finished products. (I want . . .)
4 Tom, you must deliver to the customer's home. (I told . . .)
5 You should buy in larger quantities to keep prices low. (I advise . . .)
6 You must arrange a $25,000 overdraft facility. (We expect . . .)
7 He should not believe everything they tell him. (I advised . . .)
8 She must control production. (I want . . .)
9 They must find out what the real problem is. (I told . . .)
10 This company must not lose more of its market share. (I don't want . . .)
11 He must re-consider the objectives of his company. (I advised . . .)
12 You should only buy from home suppliers. (I want . . .)

Übung 5

Verbinden Sie die zwei Satzteile mit einem Infinitiv oder mit that.

BEISPIELE   He wants / we give him the address of our agent in Denmark
He wants us to give him the address of our agent in Denmark.
We hope / they will find out the reason for the breakdown soon.
We hope that they will find out the reason for the breakdown soon.

1 I would like / you come and see me on Monday morning
2 They replied / we had more favourable prices last year
3 We told them / we had not received the letter yet
4 They want / we send them samples of the new material
5 We urged / they deliver before the introduction of new import quotas
6 She told / we be more precise in our answers
7 We hope / they will give some more detailed information
8 They advised / we advertise in trade journals

Der Infinitiv mit to in Verbindung mit for

♦ Für diese oft gebrauchte Konstruktion sind Beispiele aufgelistet.

Here are the samples for you to examine.
Hier sind die Muster, die Sie prüfen sollen.

He talks too fast for me to understand.
Er redet mir zu schnell – so schnell, daß ich nicht verstehen kann.

It is cheap enough for us to buy.
Es ist so billig, daß wir es kaufen können.

We waited for the consignment to arrive.
Wir warteten darauf, daß die Sendung kommt.

Übung 6

Vervollständigen Sie die in Klammern vorgegebenen Sätze mit der for Konstruktion und dem Infinitiv.

BEISPIEL The order is too big. We cannot complete it at such short notice. (The order is too big ...)
The order is too big for us to complete at such short notice.

1 You had better replace the faulty items. Don't wait until they complain. (Don't wait ...)
2 It is his first trip abroad. He should not go alone, it is too risky. (It is too risky ...)
3 Here is their latest balance sheet. You can study it in the plane. (Here is their latest balance sheet ...)
4 The container was too heavy. Our workers could not lift it. (The container was too heavy ...)
5 Penny knows a lot of people. She can easily work at the reception desk. (It is easy ...)
6 He should polish up his Italian. It would be useful for him. (It would be good ...)
7 They all must first learn something about management structures. (It is important ...)
8 I can't go to the bank now. It's 18.00. (It is too late ...)

Der Infinitiv ohne to

- Es handelt sich hier um einige feststehende Redewendungen *(idioms)*, die als solche zu lernen sind.

I had better	ich täte gut daran
I would rather	ich möchte lieber
I would sooner	ich möchte lieber
why not . . .	warum nicht . . .

  We had better support this product with more promotional material.
  Wir täten gut daran, den Artikel durch mehr Werbung zu unterstützen.

  Why not talk about their terms again?
  Warum (sollten wir) nicht über ihre Bedingungen erneut verhandeln?

- Der Infinitiv ohne *to* steht nach Verben des Veranlassens. Diese drei Verben werden ebenfalls am besten wie *idioms* gelernt.

  ◇ *to have sb do sth* – jdn veranlassen, etwas zu tun
  They had us increase the daily output.
  Sie veranlaßten uns, die Tagesproduktion zu erhöhen.

  ◇ *to make sb do sth* – jdn veranlassen, etwas zu tun
  He made us reduce the costs for training.
  Er veranlaßte uns, die Ausbildungskosten zu senken.

  ◇ *to let sb do sth* – jdn etwas tun lassen (im Sinne von zulassen, daß jd etwas tut)
  She let us attempt it a second time.
  Sie ließen es uns ein zweites Mal versuchen.

- Der Infinitiv ohne *to* steht nach Verben der sinnlichen Wahrnehmung *(to hear, to see, to feel, to watch, to observe, to notice)*, wenn es um kurze oder schnell aufeinanderfolgende Handlungen geht. (Vgl. Seite 126.)

  I saw her close the door.
  She saw him close his diary, get up and leave the room.

Übung 7

Setzen Sie den Infinitiv mit oder ohne to ein.

BEISPIELE   What do you advise me ... (do) in a situation like this?
What do you advise me to do in a situation like this?
It is not easy for us ... (decide) with so little information available.
It is not easy for us to decide with so little information available.
We had better ... (not interfere) in our employees' private lives.
We had better not interfere in our employees' private lives.

1 He made me ... (give) a refund to the customer.
2 She made him ...(alter) her flights because her meeting in Rome was postponed by two weeks.
3 He insisted, and so we let him ... (go) to Australia for one year.
4 I would like her ... (give) her opinion.
5 Don't make them ... (wait) too long.
6 I did not understand the text so I made them ... (translate) it for me.
7 They asked me ... (come back) after one year but I would much rather ... (stay) at our subsidiary here in Canada.
8 Mr Reade does not want anybody ... (know) about our new model.
9 If you don't know their name you had better ... (look) it up in the Yellow Pages.
10 He says we cannot do without further training. He wants us ... (attend) an evening course.
11 His secretary told us ... (come) again next Monday.
12 It is too much work for you ... (do) on your own.
13 They let us ... (go) back to work.
14 I'm sorry, but I saw you ... (pick up) the camera and ... (take) a picture. You know that's not allowed.
15 They made us ... (promise) (avoid) personal contact with our competitors' employees.
16 We would rather ... (be) second in the market with high quality goods than the market leader with cheap products.
17 They made our agent ... (stay) in a hotel because they could not find suitable accommodation for him.
18 They expect us ... (send) some information about our company.

Übung 8

Setzen Sie den Infinitiv mit oder ohne to ein.

1 They advised us . . . (lower) the prices.
2 We had better . . . (accept) his offer.
3 Why not . . . (keep) our files in alphabetical order?
4 He expected me . . . (send) it by recorded delivery.
5 They had us . . . (give) the air tickets back.
6 A new photocopier? I would rather . . . (buy) another printer.
7 They allowed him . . . (express) his opinion.
8 Why not . . . (arrange) another meeting?
9 We saw him . . . (smile) when he heard about the price reductions.
10 Mr Reade would not let the visitors . . . (see) the research and development department.
11 The security officer expects everybody . . . (observe) the safety regulations.
12 We saw the driver . . . (drop) the box.
13 The fire alarm caused the people in the training centre . . . (panic).
14 Our MD prefers us . . . (park) behind the reception building.
15 Our boss expects us . . . (meet) the deadline.
16 They made us . . . (wait) for an answer for more than two weeks.
17 We expect him . . . (arrive) at Heathrow this evening.
18 The instructor advised us not . . . (remove) the cover when the machine is working.
19 The arbitrator made him . . . (pay) the compensation back.
20 The supervisor let the female staff . . . (go) home earlier than usual.
21 The senior clerk asked the new filing clerk . . . (stop) smoking.
22 He made us . . . (leave) our cassette recorders at home because he doesn't like music in the factory.
23 I didn't notice them . . . (steal) the money from the till in the canteen.
24 We saw her . . . (retype) the letter and hurry back into Mrs Jenkins' office.

Die Vermeidung der Wiederholung eines Infinitives

♦ Ein Infinitiv, der schon genannt wurde, wird nicht wiederholt, sondern durch *to* ersetzt. Hat der Infinitiv ein Objekt, so wird dies im Wiederholungssatz weggelassen.

Tom may help her if he wants to.
We cannot give you the details although we would like to.

Übung 9

In dieser Übung finden Sie je zwei Sätze. Der Infinitiv des ersten wird im zweiten wiederholt; Sie sollen ihn jedoch durch ein einfaches to ersetzen. Meistens hat der Infinitiv ein Objekt, das lassen Sie in Ihrem zweiten Satz einfach weg.

BEISPIELE Did you work hard? Yes, I had to work hard.
Yes, I had to.
Have they answered? We asked them to reply to our letter but have not heard anything so far.
We asked them to but have not heard anything so far.

1. Did he report the matter to the security officer? No, he was too shy to report it.
2. Why did you not finish packing them? I told you to finish them.
3. Why did he not inform the foreman? He wanted to inform the foreman but he could not find him.
4. How dare you bring your radio again. You were told not to bring any radios to the factory.
5. You must visit our supplier in Croydon if you are in the area. Yes, I plan to visit him if I have time.
6. Did you lock the door? I meant to lock it but I couldn't find the key.
7. She used to have lunch with us in the canteen. I know she used to join us but now she is married and has lunch at home.
8. Why did she run out like that? She had to run because she nearly forgot her appointment with the boss.
9. Does she dance? She used to dance when she was a teenager.
10. You ought to copy the invoice. I know, I am just going to copy it.

Übersicht der Übungstypologie

Unit 1 Die Adverbien

Einführung: Adjektive und Adverbien, Einteilung der Adverbien	5
Die Stellung der bestimmten Adverbien	6
Übung 1 Einsetzübung	6
Die Stellung der unbestimmten Adverbien in einfachen Zeiten	7
Übung 2 Einsetzübung	7
Die Stellung der unbestimmten Adverbien in zusammengesetzten Zeiten	8
Übung 3 Einsetzübung	8
Die Stellung der unbestimmten Adverbien bei starker Hervorhebung	9
Übung 4 Hervorhebung durch Satzstellung	9
Die Bildung der abgeleiteten Adverbien	10
Übung 5 Bildung von Adverbien	11
Die Aufgabe der Adverbien der Art und Weise	12
Übung 6 Adjektiv und Adverb	12
Übung 7 Adjektiv oder Adverb	13
Die prädikativen Adjektive nach Verben, die keine Tätigkeit ausdrücken	13
Übung 8 Prädikatives Adjektiv oder modales Adverb	14
Die Satzfunktionen des Adverbs	14
Übung 9 Adjektive und Adverbien (in verschiedenen Funktionen)	15
Übung 10 Prädikatives und attributives Adjektiv oder Adverb	15
Reihenfolge der Adverbien im Satz	17
Übung 11 Satzstellung von Adverbien und adverbialen Bestimmungen	17
Adverbien mit Doppelformen	18
Übung 12 Einsetzen der richtigen Form	18
Im Deutschen Adverbien, im Englischen Verben	19
Übung 13 Verbale Umschreibung deutscher Adverbien	19
Zusammenfassende Übungen	20
Übung 14 Adjektiv oder Adverb, Satzstellung	20
Übung 15 Adjektiv oder Adverb	21
Übung 16 Adjektiv oder Adverb	22

Unit 2 Die indirekte Rede

Einführung	23
Die Befehlsform in der indirekten Rede	23
Übung 1 Formen des Befehls	24
Die verneinte Befehlsform	24
Übung 2 Umsetzung negativer Befehle	25
Übung 3 Umsetzung negativer und positiver Befehle	25
Übung 4 Umsetzung negativer und positiver Befehle	26
Die indirekte Rede im Aussagesatz und das Gesetz der Zeitenfolge	27
Übung 5 Anwendung auf verschiedenen Zeiten	28
Passiv und Verlaufsform in der indirekten Rede	29
Übung 6 Umsetzung von Passiv- und Verlaufsformen	29
Wortverschiebungen in der indirekten Rede	30
Übung 7 Verschiebung von Wörtern	30
Die Frage in der indirekten Rede	31
Übung 8 Umsetzung von Fragen	32
Übung 9 Umsetzung von Fragen mit Fragepronomen	32
Die Kurzantworten in der indirekten Rede	33
Übung 10 Positive und negative Kurzantworten	34
Die Hilfsverben in der indirekten Rede (*can, may, must*)	35
Übung 11 Anwendung in einfachen Zeiten	35
Zusammenfassende Übungen	36
Übung 12 Wiedergabe eines Textes	36
Übung 13 Wiedergabe eines Textes	36
Übung 14 Gemischte Übung	37

Unit 3 Das Passiv

Einführung: Bedeutung und Bildung des Passivs in allen Zeiten	38
Übung 1 Passiv in verschiedenen Zeiten	39
Das alte Subjekt des Aktivsatzes	40
Übung 2 Altes Subjekt des Aktivsatzes mit by *anfügen oder weglassen*	40
Übung 3 Übertragung eines Textes ins Passiv	41
Das Passiv bei Verben mit Präpositionen	42
Übung 4 Beibehaltung der Präposition	42
Das Passiv mit Hilfsverben	43
Übung 5 Hilfsverben in Präsens und Imperfekt	43
Übung 6 Hilfsverben in verschiedenen Zeiten	44
Übung 7 Das Passiv als Form der Höflichkeit	45
Übung 8 Voll- und Hilfsverben in verschiedenen Zeiten	46
Das Passiv bei Sätzen mit zwei Objekten	47
Übung 9 Persönliches Objekt als Subjekt des Passivsatzes	47
Das Passiv in der Verlaufsform	48
Übung 10 Anschlüsse mit when *oder* while	48
Passivkonstruktionen für das deutsche ‚man'	49
Übung 11 Das unpersönliche Passiv	50
Übung 12 Das persönliche Passiv	51
Übung 13 Gemischte Übung (alle Formen)	51
Übung 14 Rückübertragung vom Passiv ins Aktiv	52

Unit 4 Die Zeiten

Einführung	53
Die Verlaufsform: Bedeutung, Anwendung, Bildung, Zeiten	53
Übung 1 Verlaufsform mit Hilfe von Signalwörtern	54
Übung 2 Verlaufsform nach bestimmten Zeitangaben	55
Das einfache Präsens: Bedeutung und Anwendung	56
Übung 3 Einfaches Präsens oder Verlaufsform	56
Übung 4 Einfaches Präsens oder Verlaufsform	57
Übung 5 Zuordnung von Satzhälften (Einfaches Präsens oder Verlaufsform)	58
Verben, die keine Verlaufsform bilden	60
Übung 6 einfaches Präsens oder Verlaufsform	60
Die Verlaufsform im Satzgefüge	61
*Übung 7 Verlaufsform des Imperfektes (*while *und* when*)*	62
Übung 8 Zuordnung von Satzhälften (Verlaufsform oder einfaches Imperfekt)	63
Die Verlaufsform im Passiv	64
Übung 10 Gemischte Übung	65
Das Perfekt (*present perfect*): Bedeutung und Anwendung, Signalwörter	66
Since *und* for	67
Übung 11 Since *und* for	68
Übung 12 Since *und* for *als Signalwörter im Satz*	68
Das *present perfect* in der Verlaufsform	69
Übung 13 Einfaches present perfect *oder Verlaufsform des* present perfect	69
Das Imperfekt (*simple past*): Bedeutung und Anwendung, Signalwörter	70
Übung 14 simple past *oder* present perfect *mit vorgegebenen Signalwörtern*	70
Übung 15 simple past *oder* present perfect *mit Signalwörtern*	71
Übung 16 simple past *oder* present perfect	72
*Übung 17 Zuordnung von Satzhälften (*simple past *oder* present perfect*)*	73
Übung 18 Zusammenfassende Übung (verschiedene Zeiten)	74

Übersicht der Übungstypologie | 149

Unit 5 Die Konditionalsätze (if-Sätze)

Einführung: Konditionalsätze und ihre Bedeutungen (die drei Typen von *if*-Sätzen)	75
Übung 1 Schematische Anwendung mit Vorgabe des Typenschemas	76
Übung 2 Ergänzung des Typenschemas	77
Übung 3 Bildung aller drei Typen von if-Sätzen	78
Übung 4 Bildung von Typ 3	78
Übung 5 Ergänzung bei Vorgaben verschiedener Zeiten	79
Übung 6 Bildung von Typ 3 bei Vorgabe von zwei Einzelsätzen	80
Der Gebrauch von *was* und *were* im *if*-Satz	81
Übung 7 Schematische Übung (If I was/were you ...)	81
Übung 8 Bildung aller drei Typen (alle Zeitformen)	82
Die unvollständigen Hilfsverben im *if*-Satz	83
Übersicht über die vereinfachten Anwendungsformen	83
Übung 9 Anwendung vereinfachter Formen	84
Übung 10 Einsetzen von Passivformen in Konditionalstrukturen	85
Übung 11 Verschiedene Formen im Sachzusammenhang	86

Unit 6 Die modalen Hilfsverben

Einführung	87
Können, Möglichkeit, Erlaubnis: Bedeutung und Formen (*can, could, to be able to*)	88
Übung 1 Umschreibungsform (to be able to) *in allen Zeiten*	89
Übung 2 Einsetzen einer passenden Zeitform	89
Erlaubnis, Möglichkeit, Verbot: Bedeutung und Formen (*may, might, to be allowed to, must not*)	90
Übung 3 Umschreibungsformen in allen Zeiten	91
Übung 4 Einsetzen passender Hilfsverben oder deren Umschreibungen	92
Übung 5 Gemischte Übung (Einsetzen passender Formen vorgegebener Verben)	93
Zwang, Notwendigkeit: Bedeutung und Formen (*must, to have to*)	94
Übung 6 Anwendung von to have to in allen Zeiten	95
Übung 7 Kombination von zusammengehörigen Zeiten	95
Der verneinte Zwang: Bedeutung und Formen (*don't have to, need not, don't need to*)	97
Übung 8 Die drei Formen des Nichtbrauchens im Präsens	97
Übung 9 don't have to *in verschiedenen Zeiten*	98
Zwei schwierigere Formen des verneinten Zwangs (*did not have to, need not have*)	98
Übung 10 Erschließen der richtigen Form aus dem Kontext	99
Verbot und verneinter Zwang: Bedeutung (*must not, need not*)	100
Übung 11 Erschließen der richtigen Form aus dem Kontext	100
Die Frage nach einem Zwang oder einer Notwendigkeit: Formen und Zeiten (*do I have to, need I, do I need to, have I got to, must I*)	101
Übung 12 to have to *in der Frage in verschiedenen Zeiten*	101
Sollen: englische Entsprechungen (*shall, should, ought to, to be supposed to*)	102
Übung 13 Sollen mit vorgegebem Sinn	102
Übung 14 Erschließen der richtigen Form aus dem Kontext	103
To be said to als Wiedergabe von Gerüchten oder Vermutungen	104
Übung 15 Erschließen der richtigen Wendungen aus dem Kontext	104
Wollen: englische Entsprechungen (*to wish, to be willing to, to intend to, to mean to, to want*)	105
Übung 16 Wollen mit vorgegebenem Sinn	106
Übung 17 Zusammenfassende Übung	106

Unit 7 Das Gerundium

Einführung: Bedeutung und Formen	108
Das Gerundium als Subjekt	110
Übung 1 Verwandlung von Infinitiven in Gerundien	110
Das Gerundium als logisches Subjekt	111
Übung 2 Infinitiv oder Gerundium	111
Das Gerundium als direktes Objekt	112
Verben, die das Gerundium verlangen	113
Verben, die Gerundium und Infinitiv zulassen	113
Übung 3 Bildung von Gerundien nach Vorgaben	114
Das Gerundium als prädikative Ergänzung	115
Übung 4 Einsetzen der Gerundien nach Vorgaben	115
Das Gerundium als präpositionale Ergänzung	116
Übung 5 Einsetzen gerundialer Formen mit vorgegebenen präpositionalen Wendungen	118
Übung 6 Zuordnung von Satzhälften	119
Übung 7 Einsetzen von Präposition und Gerundium	119
Das Gerundium als adverbiale Bestimmung	120
Übung 8 Bildung von Gerundien nach Vorgaben	120
Übung 9 Verwendung des Gerundiums anstelle eines Adverbialsatzes	121
Das Gerundium mit eigenem Subjekt	122
Übung 10 Ersetzen von Nebensätzen (Objektsätzen) durch Gerundien	122
Übung 11 Gemischte Übung	123

Unit 8 Das Partizip

Einführung: Bedeutung und Formen	124
Das Partizip als Ergänzung zum Subjekt	125
Übung 1 Einsetzen eines auszuwählenden Verbs in partizipialer Form	125
Das Partizip als Ergänzung zum direkten Objekt	126
Übung 2 Einsetzen des Infinitivs oder Partizips vorgegebener Verben	126
Übung 3 Einsetzen von Verben der sinnlichen Wahrnehmung und Infinitiv oder Partizip	127
Lassen (*to leave, to keep*) und Veranlassen	128
Übung 4 Einsetzen partizipialer Formen von vorgegebenen Verben	128
Übung 5 Einsetzen des Verben des Lassens und Veranlassens	129
Übung 6 Einsetzen von Partizip Präsens oder Partizip Perfekt	129
Das Partizip in der Funktion eines Relativsatzes	130
Übung 7 Partizipien als Ersatz für Relativsätze	130
Das Partizip als verkürzter Adverbialsatz	131
Übung 8 Ersetzen des adverbialen Nebensatzes durch Partizipialkonstruktionen	132
Übung 9 Einsetzen der verschiedenen Zeitformen des Partizips	133
Partizipialsätze mit einleitenden Konjunktionen	134
Übung 10 Auswahl einer von drei vorgebenen Konjunktionen	134
Partizipialkonstruktionen mit eigenem Subjekt	135
Übung 11 Einsetzen von with *mit eingeleiteten unverbundenen Partizipien*	135
Übung 12 Gemischte Übung (alle bekannten Partizipialkonstruktionen)	136

Unit 9 Der Infinitiv

Einführung: Bedeutung und Formen	137
Der Infinitiv mit *to* (Überblick)	138
Der Infinitiv mit *to* als Attribut (nach Substantiven, Adjektiven und superlativischen Wendungen, Ordnungszahlen und *only*)	138
Übung 1 Der Infinitiv mit to *als Attribut zu Adjektiven*	139
Übung 2 Der Infinitiv mit to *als Attribut nach superlativischen Wendungen, Ordnungszahlen und* only	139
Der Infinitiv mit *to* nach *how, what, when, who, which* und *whether*	140
Übung 3 Der Infinitiv mit Fragewort statt eines Nebensatzes	140
Der Infinitiv mit *to* als indirekter Befehl (Verb+Obj.+Infinitiv mit *to*)	141
Übung 4 Infinitiv mit to *als indirekter Befehl*	142
Übung 5 Infinitiv oder Nebensatz mit that	142
Der Infinitiv mit *to* in Verbindung mit *for*	143
Übung 6 Schematische Übung	143
Der Infinitiv ohne *to*	144
Übung 7 Infinitiv mit oder ohne to	145
Übung 8 Infinitiv mit oder ohne to	146
Die Vermeidung der Wiederholung eines Infinitives	147
Übung 9 Bildung verkürzter Sätze	147

Business Grammar Intermediate

Schlüssel

1 Die Adverbien

Übung 1
(Lösungsvorschlag)
1. ... in business since 1920.
2. ... a subsidiary in Wales.
3. ... their branches from their headquarters.
4. In the early eighties Mr Reade thought ...
5. ... was gradually reduced during the recession.
6. During the last five years 20 per cent ...
7. ... had to be made on the managerial level, too.
8. ... was rather cool at the Annual General Meeting.
9. ... will have expanded considerably by the end of the year.
10. ... will increase in the next decade.
11. ... a board meeting every week.
12. ... was fixed this morning.
13. ... has worked very hard today.
14. ... work by six o'clock.

Übung 2
1. politely invites
2. always offer
3. urgently requested
4. frequently tried
5. certainly thinks
6. regularly send
7. reluctantly agreed
8. clearly show
9. wisely invited
10. always consults
11. patiently explained
12. finally found
13. impatiently asked
14. immediately admitted
15. kindly offered

Übung 3
1. is always the first
2. has carefully set aside
3. are easily dealt with
4. is sometimes a little
5. would considerably speed up
6. is always Penny
7. is always friendly
8. is always attached
9. should be clearly stamped
10. has carefully sorted
11. Having quickly done
12. is sometimes addressed

Übung 4
1. Fortunately she returned ...
2. ... twice this morning already.
   oder He has already shouted ...
3. Wisely they will try ...
4. ... to start work more punctually.
5. ... every paragraph of the contract carefully.
   oder Mr Reade has carefully read ...
6. Certainly it will be finished ...
7. You can easily find ...
8. Perhaps he has thrown it ...
9. She is nervously looking ...
10. Tom is always willing ...
11. Mrs Jenkins often prefers ...
    oder Often Mrs Jenkins prefers ...
12. They willingly accepted ...
    oder ... our suggestions willingly.

Übung 5
1. fully
2. readily
3. confidentially
4. completely
5. in a friendly way
6. politely
7. possibly
8. decidedly
9. well
10. remarkably
11. duly
12. Strictly

Übung 6
1. accurately
2. well
3. happily
4. patiently
5. fluently
6. seriously
7. in a friendly way
8. comfortably
9. entirely
10. carelessly
11. kindly
12. slowly, carefully

Übung 7
1. intelligent
2. punctually
3. quickly
4. politely
5. unexpected
6. thoroughly
7. trustworthy
8. complete
9. unexpectedly
10. generous
11. democratically
12. careful

Übung 8
1. fine
2. immediately
3. calm
4. enthusiastically
5. aggressive
6. excellent
7. carefully
8. polite
9. sad
10. mutual

Übung 9
1. terribly tired
2. really
3. probably
4. particularly careful
5. extremely irritable
6. highly sensitive
7. perhaps, immediately
8. kindly

Übung 10
1. particularly, particular, particular, particularly
2. remarkable, remarkably, remarkable
3. Usually, usual, usually, usually
4. highly, high, highly, high
5. generally, general, generally, general
6. safe, safely, safe
7. main, mainly, mainly

Übung 11
1. We are certainly going to the export fair next week.
   oder Certainly we are going to the export fair next week.
2. We will probably stay there for the rest of the week.
3. Mr Reade likes a cup of tea early in the morning.
4. I'm sorry, but my bus was late this morning.
5. You can meet Mr Reade at our stand between 3 and 4 o'clock every afternoon.
6. I talked to him in his office yesterday.
   oder I talked to him yesterday in his office.
7. He was on the continent several times last year.
8. She spends most of her time in the design room at her computer.
   oder ... at her computer in the design room.
9. We will meet him at the airport at 9.15 a.m. tomorrow morning.
   oder ... at the airport tomorrow morning at 9.15 a.m.
10. He is already preparing to go home.
    oder He is preparing to go home already.
11. We will get a lot of orders and find new customers at the trade fair in London next month.
12. He finds that, above all before Christmas, demand often exceeds supply in the high-street branches.
    oder He finds that demand often exceeds supply in the high-street branches, above all before Christmas.
13. He never comes to the office before nine in the morning.
14. We always have our Christmas dinner at the five-star hotel in town.

Übung 12
1. lately
2. hardly
3. lately
4. just

5 late
6 just
7 hardly
8 late

Übung 13
1 They happened to meet ...
2 I (We) hope they will get on ...
3 ... but seem to be good workers.
4 They continue to send ...
5 I prefer to meet ...
6 I (We) suppose (presume) she will be ...
7 I'm sorry (I'm afraid) I cannot pass on ...
8 He always prefers to stay ...
9 I (We) hope the goods in transport were ...
10 Our new customer seems to be ...

Übung 14
1 They found our suggestions unacceptable.
2 The number of telex machines is decreasing steadily in modern offices.
   oder ... is steadily decreasing in modern offices.
3 Our budgeted sales performance differs slightly from our real overall sales performance.
4 He cut him short angrily.
5 Unfortunately the morning is booked up, but the early afternoon would be convenient.
   oder The morning is unfortunately booked up, but ...
6 High street prices are falling sharply because of the recession.
7 All our questions were answered clearly.
   oder All our questions were clearly answered.
8 It has been a terribly busy morning so far.
   oder So far it has been a terribly busy morning.
9 To cut a long story short, our sales figures must improve considerably.
10 Market research and sales promotion are regarded as equally essential in our firm.
11 This problem must be solved urgently.
12 He always thinks field research causes unnecessary expenses.
13 He pointed furiously at the gap between the two lines on the graph.
14 We ran short of our pocket models just before sales started.
   oder Just before sales started, we ran short of ...
15 They are always punctual in settling their accounts.
16 They produce them at a relatively high cost.
17 It was a most profitable deal.
18 We priced our export models independently from our models for the domestic market.
19 The cheap model is really easy to handle.
20 Privatized enterprises have not always proved to be efficient.

Übung 15
1 completely
2 considerably
3 strange
4 clearly
5 chaotic
6 brisk
7 surprisingly
8 profitable
9 traditional
10 lately
11 hardly, hard
12 large
13 considerably
14 completely
15 high
16 suspiciously
17 badly
18 impartially
19 effectively
20 economical

Übung 16
1 Originally
2 frequently
3 later
4 highly
5 particular
6 generally
7 hardly
8 understandable
9 strictly
10 honestly
11 really
12 financial
13 seriously
14 exact
15 considerably

2 Die indirekte Rede

Übung 1

1. He asked me to come ...
   He said I should come ...
2. He urged her to write ...
   He said she should write ...
3. She asked me to hold it for her.
   She said I should hold ...
4. He urged us to despatch ...
   He said we should despatch ...
5. He advised me to offer ...
   He said I should offer ...
6. They advised Mr. Reade to increase ...
   They said Mr. Reade should increase ...
7. She urged him to give reasons for his demand.
   She said he should give ...
8. They asked them to improve ...
   They said they should improve ...
9. We asked them to give ...
   We said they should give ...
10. He advised us to present ...
    They said we should present ...
11. They advised us to advertise ...
    They said we should advertise ...
12. He told me to organize ...
    He said I should organize ...
13. They encouraged us to introduce ...
    They said we should introduce ...
14. I advised them to rationalize their filing system.
    I said they should rationalize ...
15. He urged us to train ...
    He said we should train ...
16. He encouraged us to spend ...
    He said we should spend ...
17. He told them to replace ...
    He said they should replace ...
18. I encouraged them to build up ...
    I said they should build up ...

Übung 2

(Lösungsvorschlag)

1. Mrs Jenkins asked us not to keep her ...
2. Our accountant told me not to hesitate ...
3. Bill warned me not to go ...
4. Our shop steward ordered us not to do ...
5. They urged me not to be ...
6. She begged me not to lose my temper ...
7. He encouraged me not to turn her down ...
8. The architect advised us not to locate ...
9. Our buyer requested us not to look ...
10. Susan forbade him to accept ...

Übung 3

(Die einführenden Satzteile sind beliebig.)

1. She told us not to hold the receiver in the hand we ...
2. We were advised to give our ...
3. She said we should use ...
4. She warned us not to keep ...
5. She told us not to argue but to be ...
6. We were warned never to put ...
7. She said we should write down ...
8. She advised us to read back ...
9. She said we should offer to ring back if we ...
10. We were told not to forget ...
11. She advised us to take down ...
12. We were told to apologize if we ...
13. She told us never to give ...
14. She said we should reassure ...

Übung 4

(Lösungsvorschlag)

1. We were advised to unplug ...
2. We were told never to use ...
3. We were warned not to place ...

4   We were told to transport ...
5   They said we should cover ...
6   I learnt that we should never block ...
7   We were told to check ...
8   They said we should never use ...
9   We were told to place ...
10 We were warned not to attempt to service the printer ourselves.

Übung 5

1   He said that the company had been ...
2   He added that they had planned ...
3   He admitted that some of their goods were ...
4   They realized that their stockholding costs had been ...
5   He added that there hadn't been ...
6   He said that he had had ...
7   He told me that he had been made ...
8   He said that he would apply ...
9   He promised that he was ...
10 He wanted to know if (whether) there were ...
11 She confirmed that their advertising campaign had been ...
12 She admitted that there had been ...
13 She said that all our sales literature had got ...
14 She assured us that they had always complied ...
15 She repeated that all the advertising material was ...
16 She was sure that all orders would be met ...
17 She explained that she wanted ...
18 She added that they had given ...
19 She said that they always offered ...
20 She drew Tom's attention to the fact that the other firm had so far only sold ...

Übung 6
(Die einführenden Satzteile sind beliebig.)

1   She said that Penny's replacement was going to type ...
2   He told us that he was going to meet ...
3   The managing director said that he would not be moved ...
4   She said that he was having ...
5   I told the sales manager that I had been checking the sales figures and that she had been working ...
6   The receptionist said that the visitor had been waiting ...
7   He told the board that the loss had been offset ...
8   She said that the conditions of the contract had been examined.
9   The secretary said that the invitations were just being typed.
10 She said she was going to take part ...
11 She said she was correcting ...
12 He said that he had been working ...

Übung 7
(Lösungsvorschlag)

1   They said that they had received our consignment the day before.
2   She remarked that she was positive that the meeting that day would be a short one.
3   We heard that the company had always been based there.
4   She explained that she had filed her tax return the week before.
5   He stated that she had applied for the job three weeks before, but had not turned up for the interview.
6   We heard that the complaint had been settled by arbitration the previous week.
7   They promised that they had finished the shortlist and were preparing the schedule for the interviews that day.
8   She explained that they had not got any details then.

9. She remarked that they were talking about a strike then but that they had not considered the long-term effect.
10. He stated that he would not have the results till the following week.
11. She remarked that those items were very reasonably priced.
12. We added that we would cancel our contract with them the following day if they did not give any reasons for the delay.
13. He stated that he would not reject that offer.
14. They promised that the invoice had been settled about six weeks before.
15. She explained that the consignment they had received the day before, was (had been) three weeks late.
    (Vermeiden Sie ein doppeltes Plusquamperfekt.)
16. She explained that it meant that they would have to do overtime the following month.

Übung 8
(Die Personal-und Possessivpronomen sind beliebig.)
1. He asked if (whether) recession was ...
2. She asked if (whether) we had chosen ...
3. He asked if (whether) they had ...
4. He asked if (whether) she already knew ...
5. She asked if (whether) he was ...
6. They asked if (whether) they could have ...
7. He asked if (whether) he could ... *oder* He asked if (whether) he might ...
8. She asked if (whether) the time suited ...
9. He asked if (whether) the cheque was ...
10. We asked if (whether) they charged ...
11. She asked if (whether) I had put in ...
12. She asked if (whether) we had received ...
13. He asked if (whether) we could calculate ...
14. They asked if (whether) their account would be ...
15. He asked if (whether) the expenses had been refunded.

Übung 9
(Die Personal-und Possessivpronomen sind beliebig.)
1. They asked how they could cut down on travel costs.
2. She asked what he had said during the meeting.
3. He asked where I had put the previous month's figures.
4. She asked what I thought of their new SX models.
5. She asked what skills were needed for that job.
6. He asked what the unemployment situation in my part of the country was like.
7. He asked how long I had been working for them.
8. He asked how many workers they employed.
9. I asked where the company had its headquarters.
10. He asked what they had offered during the negotiations.
11. She asked when they had filed for bankruptcy.
12. They asked what percentage of the costs advertising accounted for.
13. They asked where they could get the proposal forms.
14. She asked how she could get in touch with him.
15. They asked when the difficulties had started.
16. He asked what their complaint was about.
17. She asked what our area code was.
18. She asked what number I had dialled.

Übung 10
1 ... if (whether) we had offered them a $2,000 credit. / ... that we hadn't.
2 ... if (whether) we would come to an agreement with them. / ... that we would.
3 ... if (whether) the goods had found a market. / ... that they had.
4 ... if (whether) that was an order for immediate delivery. / ... that it was.
5 ... if (whether) they had submitted an offer. / ... that they hadn't.
6 ... if (whether) we were satisfied with their rates of pay. / ... that we were.
7 ... if (whether) our sales figures in that area would recover. / ... that they would.
8 ... if (whether) we were satisfied with the results. / ... that we were.
9 ... if (whether) there had been any complaint about the sample. / ... that there had.
10 ... if (whether) there would be a delay in delivery. / ... that there wouldn't.
11 ... if (whether) they had made the necessary arrangements. / ... that they had.
12 ... if (whether) we could hold the goods for ten days. / ... that we could.

Übung 11
(Die einführenden Satzteile sind beliebig)
1 They said that they were not able to (could not) rent ...
2 They said that they had to charge ...
3 She said that they needed her there, so she was not able to (could not) help ...
4 I said that she had to leave if she wanted ...
5 He said that I was not allowed to take ...
6 They said that they had been able (would be able) to reduce ...
7 They said that they had to launch ...
8 They said that it was an introductory price and that they were not able to (could not) tell us what the final price would be.
9 They said that they had to update ...
10 They said that their service electrician had not been able to carry out ...
11 They said that they had to find someone who spoke ...
12 He said that he had not been able to start ...

Übung 12
(Lösungsvorschlag)
... a deal had been struck between trade unions and the Post Office that would allow postmen to wear shorts. Although, it was admitted that there were some postmen who had been wearing them for years already, this was the first time that shorts had been accepted as part of the postmen's dresscode. It was said that shorts would be allowed if the temperature went above 78°F. It was explained, however, that the shorts that were permitted had to be dark and of Bermuda-length rather than running shorts. They said that in that way it was guaranteed that the shorts would be in keeping with the rest of the uniform. It was made clear that a postman wearing lilac beach shorts would not be allowed to go on his round.

Übung 13
(Lösungsvorschlag)
Our computer teacher informed us today that there were some computers which could only do word processing. He told us that there were two basic types. He said that a stand-alone system was intended for one operator only and could process texts, whereas a communicating and shared-logic system, however, kept several operators at different keyboards busy. He added that each of them had access to a central hard-disk.

He explained that wordprocessors could perform many different sorts of office work: files could be stored on floppy disks or on a central hard-disk. He told us that once a document had been keyed in and stored, it could be called up on the screen and worked on. He said that old information could be removed and new paragraphs could be added. The teacher added that the layout of a letter could be altered without difficulty. He remarked that any data stored or loaded into the computer's memory could be combined with an already existing text and that the screen would show you exactly what the wordprocessor was going to print.

Übung 14
(Die einführenden Satzteile sind beliebig.)

1 He said that the trial order had been completed ...
2 They complained that they had to invest ...
3 We agreed that Penny had not been wrong ...
4 She warned us that train connections to Mid-Wales were ...
5 They stated that they had been ...
6 They said that they were going to launch ...
7 They admitted that that they would have to cut back ...
8 They added that even their competitors said that their new line was ...
9 He said that he expected to come ...
10 They admitted that they would have to overcome ...
11 He insisted that their agent was most certainly not going to offer ...
12 He said that he did not think it was ...
13 He told them that the decisions they had to make required ...
14 He complained that it had taken him six months to find ...
15 He explained that three years before Susan had worked ...
16 He explained that at breakeven point you neither earned a profit nor suffered ...
17 He told Tom that he had to provide ...
18 He informed them that they had to try ...

3 Das Passiv

Übung 1
1. will be settled, has been settled
2. would be cancelled, would have been cancelled
3. is rejected, was rejected
4. will be finished, had been finished
5. had been discussed, would have been discussed
6. will be installed, was installed
7. has not been solved, would not be solved

Übung 2
1. Our line managers are kept informed.
2. Several changes were suggested.
3. Distribution has been improved considerably by computers.
4. Have the goods been packed?
5. These cases have been put on the lorries.
6. Goods are bought in great quantities.
7. The goods are held, until they are asked for.
8. In this way a steady flow of production is kept up.
9. All the faulty cars were recalled.
10. That is why predictions about the market are needed.
11. First components were produced, then machines were manufactured, now complete systems are offered.
12. Raw materials will be traded in for high quality western products.
13. The agreement was interpreted in a different way.
14. That point will be put on the agenda.
15. A furious reaction will probably be triggered by this product.
16. His report was submitted to the board two weeks ago.
17. A substantial contract for office furniture was won by our company.
18. The ideas have been discussed by the committee.
19. The chairperson will be elected by the Board of Directors.
20. The goods will be sent to you on Friday.

Übung 3
Goods are bought in bulk from the manufacturer by the wholesaler.[1] They are kept in stock[2] until they are required by the retailer.[3] Of course a fee is charged for this service,[4] i.e. the selling price is raised.[5]
The wholesaler's part is often considered unnecessary.[6] In fact, however, both the manufacturer and the retailer are helped by the wholesaler.[7] The flow of goods between manufacturers and retailers has always been controlled by wholesalers.[8] The manufacturer's costs are reduced by the wholesaler[9] as he reduces the need to store finished products in warehouses. Retailers like this arrangement because goods can be bought in smaller quantities.[10]
In many cases credit is offered to the retailers by wholesalers[11] so that they do not have to look for loans elsewhere. But the wholesaler's position has been weakened by the modern economy.[12] His or her importance has been reduced by new methods of distribution.[13] The wholesaler has been eliminated completely by many manufacturers through direct selling.[14]

Übung 4
1. His appointment was approved of.
2. When should he be picked up from his hotel?
3. Who was the lorry hired from?
4. Why has an insurance policy not been taken out?
5. A lot of notice was taken of this new material.

6 Who was he recommended to?
7 A lot of attention is paid to sales exhibitions.
8 Has the question of the new markets in eastern Europe been brought up?
9 The new photocopier is made use of by all of them.
10 The misprints in our new catalogue were laughed at.
11 Her youth was taken account of in her appraisal.
12 Who was the letter addressed to?
13 What has Penny been congratulated on?
14 All I can see is his incompetence and that is not what he is paid for.
15 Will the sales trainees be looked after properly?

Übung 5
1 An advertisement had to be placed ...
2 ... that in-company recruitment could not be considered.
3 A detailed job description had to be provided by Miss Powell.
4 Our company's general application form could be used.
5 A reference had to be written ...
6 All the references ought to be checked by Ruth ...
7 Four candidates can be short-listed.
8 Appointments must be arranged ...
9 Four members may be selected for the interview panel by Mr Reade.
10 A contract of employment has to be prepared by our personnel department.

Übung 6
Letter of inquiry
1 Can a delivery date be fixed by the supplier.
2 Is credit offered?
3 More than one letter of inquiry will be written by a customer.
4 Thus goods and prices can be compared.

Quotation
5 A quotation will be sent by the potential supplier.
6 The terms of trade might be found in a price-list by the potential customer.
7 ... i.e. the price that has to be paid by the consumer.
8 A trade discount will be offered by the supplier.
9 It is a reduction that is granted by the manufacturer.
10 In this way a profit can be made by the retailer.
11 ... bulk or quantity discounts might be granted by the supplier.

Terms of Delivery
12 The cost of transportation will be paid for by the supplier.
13 A fee for delivery has to be paid by the customer.
14 The buyer is charged by the manufacturer with ...
15 The cost of delivery to the railway terminal nearest the seller is included in the quoted price.
16 A price is stated by the seller that includes delivery to the dockside. Freight, insurance and loading charges are taken care of by the buyer.
17 The charge for the loading is paid by the seller as well.
18 Delivery to the dockside and loading and freight charges to the customer's port are included in the seller's price.
19 The costs for insurance to the port destination are also paid by the seller.
20 The unloading charges at the port destination are also included in the exporter's price.
21 All the charges are paid by the seller and he delivers ...

Terms of payment
22 An invoice is usually sent in advance of delivery by the seller.
23 The goods will only be shipped when ...

24 The carrier must be paid in cash by the buyer.
25 Special credit terms can be agreed (upon) by both parties.
26 The buyer will always be encouraged to pay promptly by the seller.
27 Cash discounts have always been offered by sellers for ...
28 Thus the trouble of sending reminders is avoided.

Übung 7
1 This mistake has been made ...
2 The terms of payment were misunderstood.
3 The goods should have been examined ...
4 Apparently our operating instructions have not been read.
5 A mistake was made when the consignment was prepared ...
6 The cupboards we did not order must be collected.
7 The whole order will be cancelled if it is not delivered ...
8 Our order will be placed elsewhere if we are informed that it cannot be completed ...
9 We realize that quite a number of mistakes were made.
10 The unbelievable sum of $3,000 has been charged for equipment that was not ordered.
11 The problem must be solved ...
12 An explanation should be given.
13 The matter must be looked into ...
14 The letter should have been sent ...

Übung 8
1 The breakeven point must be reached ...
2 Our department has been equipped ...
3 Where should the new department be based?
4 All our capital would be tied up by this new machine.
5 Our last invoice has not yet been paid.
6 A shortlist of candidates that are suitable for the position will be drawn up.
7 So far only one third of the applicants has been interviewed.
8 The two alternatives will have to be weighed up.
9 The faulty CD players will be exchanged ...
10 The damaged parts had to be replaced ...
11 Only conditions that compare favourably with those of our competitors will be accepted.
12 Our interests there must be represented by our agent there.
13 The loss would be covered.
14 A meeting is controlled by a chairperson.
15 Our operating instructions will have to be followed ...
16 His name was never mentioned ...

Übung 9
1 Non-members were denied the right ...
2 Bill Mitchell has been made shop steward.
3 She was offered a room ...
4 The new shop-steward was given the key ...
5 Bill was handed a box ...
6 ... that she had not been granted her sick pay.
7 ... that she had been refused a day off for her sister's wedding.
8 Sarah was not shown the confidential report.
9 ... because his younger colleague had been offered higher wages.
10 The secretary had obviously not been shown her job appraisal.
11 ... that they had been promised better lighting, but ...
12 Bill was offered a more senior position ...

Lösungen

Übung 10

1. Our new product was just being launched when ...
2. The assembly line was being cleaned while ...
3. The delivery note was being typed when ...
4. The rest of the burnt cases were being examined by the insurance agent while ...
5. She was being trained for the position of personal assistant while ...
6. The paintbrushes were being offered at reduced prices when ...
7. The typewriter was being cleaned when ...
8. The goods they had ordered the week before were being delivered when ...
9. The secretaries were being informed when ...
10. Our new branch in Togo was just being set up when ...
11. A new production line was being set up when ...
12. He was being retrained for another job while ...
13. The stock room was being prepared for the goods when ...
14. The quotation is being checked while ...

Übung 11

1. It is supposed that ...
2. It is generally assumed that ...
3. It is said that ...
4. It is assumed that ...
5. It is feared that ...
6. It is said that ...
7. It is believed that ...
8. It is said that ...
9. It is said that ...
10. It is believed that ...

Übung 12

1. She is said to be ...
2. She is assumed to have applied for ...
3. He is said to be ...
4. Thousands of investors are believed to have lost ...
5. They are known to carry out ...
6. He is said to be ...
7. His job is supposed to be ...
8. We are expected to have ...
9. She is said to keep ...
10. They are known to pay ...

Übung 13

1. This meeting has been called to look into ...
2. A lot of attention was paid to ...
3. The list is going to be checked.
4. Penny was treated to a snack by Tom.
5. We were offered payment by ...
   oder Payment was offered by ...
6. Why was it mentioned ...
7. ... a change in leadership had been expected.
8. Prices had been carefully compared before the order was placed.
9. Several substantial orders have been secured ...
10. The fax machine must have been connected ...
11. It is to be expected that the mislaid contract will be found by the secretary.
    oder The secretary is expected to find ...
12. He can be given ...
13. The problem was explained to us by the chairperson.
14. A lot of attention was paid to ...
15. It is assumed that ...
16. Our contract with them can be cancelled ...
17. The goods had been ordered ...
18. Delegating is said to be ...

19. Express delivery was promised to our new customers.
    oder Our new customers were promised ...
20. A mistake has been made ...
21. A breakdown in communication must be avoided.
22. The organization is being analyzed (by these people).
23. No notice was taken of the memo.
    oder The memo was not taken any notice of.
24. It is believed that ...
25. In this way our marketing costs will be reduced.
26. The annual results are just being announced.

Übung 14
(Lösungsvorschlag)

1. They do not fully train these new agents.
2. We did not accept their proposal.
3. They have always given us good service.
4. They will transfer him ...
5. We will meet the target date ...
6. I think we can persuade him ...
7. You must do all this ...
8. We must renegotiate the prices.
9. ... we could supply no more than 30% of the order.
10. We will leave contract negotiations to Mrs Jenkins.
11. They are just preparing the annual accounts.
12. You can reduce transit time if ...
13. They will transfer the goods ...
14. We will have to place the goods ...

4 Die Zeiten

Übung 1
1. Look, Tom is opening ...
2. Now he is distributing ...
3. At the moment he is emptying ...
4. Now he is helping ...
5. He is worried; he is looking ...
6. He is just collecting ...
7. Look at Tom, he is putting ...
8. He is sealing ...
9. He is going ...
10. Now he is helping out ...

Übung 2
1. She is preparing ...
2. She is taking ...
3. She is ringing
4. They are both having ...
5. Mrs Jenkins is talking ...
6. Susan is keying ...
7. Susan is going ...
8. She is receiving ...

Übung 3
1. employs
2. is working
3. are advertising
4. interview *oder* are interviewing
5. switch
6. is having
7. are offering
8. are having
9. is chairing
10. provides
11. is he staying
12. am retyping
13. is showing
14. does he want
15. is expecting
16. does one box contain

Übung 4
1. A What do top executives do?
   B plan, carry out
2. A belongs
   B make
3. B looks after, sorts out, checks
4. A is just staring, is not doing
   B is checking up
5. A are working
   B is talking
6. A is wearing, (is) standing
   A is he doing
   B do not know, is listening
7. B is going, (is) collecting
   A happens
   B takes, hands
8.   does
   B usually do
   P work, am typing
9. A is just crossing
   B is having
10.   meets
    A are you waiting
    P am waiting, have

Übung 5
3 b, 4 a
5 b, 6 a
7 a, 8 b
9 b, 10 a
11 a, 12 b
13 b, 14 a
15 b, 16 a
17 a, 18 b
19 a, 20 b
21 b, 22 a

Übung 6
1. wants
2. needs
3. agree
4. belongs
5. hope *oder* are hoping

6 smoke
7 is signing
8 is listening, agrees
9 regret
10 think
11 are having
12 have
13 do not deal
14 have, knows
15 is ringing
16 is boarding
17 do you have
18 renew
19 inspect
20 not like, doubt

Übung 7
1 were you sitting, was standing
2 was travelling, were preparing
3 was sitting
4 were they doing, were looking
5 was planning
6 were you waiting
7 was preparing, was interviewing
8 was accessing
9 was waiting
10 was discussing, was noting down
11 were you doing, was playing
12 were they drinking, were celebrating
13 were you doing, were celebrating
14 were working
15 were they discussing

Übung 8
1 b, 2 a
3 b, 4 a
5 b, 6 a
7 a, 8 b
9 b, 10 a
11 a, 12 b

Übung 9
1 are being introduced
2 is being interviewed
3 were being studied
4 is being assembled
5 are being tested
6 were being checked
7 is being offered
8 was being introduced

Übung 10
1 takes
2 am thinking
3 are talking
4 is being prepared
5 is working, is she doing, is counting
6 is still studying
7 was being programmed
8 contains
9 is writing
10 wants
11 was he doing
12 was taking
13 meet
14 doubt
15 know
16 raises *oder* raised
17 talks, finds
18 was replacing
19 makes
20 set up
21 works, is spending
22 found, was having

Übung 11
1 since
2 for
3 for
4 since
5 for
6 for
7 since
8 for
9 for
10 since
11 for
12 since

Übung 12
1 ... since the Industrial Revolution./ ... for the last hundred years.
2 ... since they were introduced onto the market./... for more than 10 years.
3 ... for two months./... since we dismissed their complaint.

4 ... since the expansion of our production department./... for 10 years.
5 ... for the last two years./... since the merger with Distribution International Ltd.
6 ... since we moved into our new building./... for at least two years.
7 ... for longer than I can remember./... since the mid-eighties.
8 ... for the last three months./... since we gave up ordering the files chronologically.

Übung 13

1 have always contained
2 has been checking
3 has been querying
4 have belonged
5 has been
6 have been looking, have still not found
7 has been filing
8 has been
9 have been planning
10 have always used
11 have been
12 have not seen
13 have decided
14 have agreed
15 have been
16 have been working-to-rule

Übung 14

1 telephoned
2 called back
3 has greatly reduced
4 proposed
5 used
6 has not gone up
7 has gone down
8 has never lost
9 have gone up
10 have never bought
11 supplied
12 marketed
13 forgot
14 has not looked
15 has soared

Übung 15

1 Last year they exported 80% of their production.
2 They have sold only brushes and rollers so far.
3 It's only October and their turnover has doubled this year.
4 Many orders came in in their first year of trading.
5 Their business has grown considerably since then.
6 We have had no letters today – perhaps some will come by second delivery.
7 He secured many orders when he was new at the job.
8 We closed the agreement last month.
9 They paid him extra commission last year.
10 She has lived in Belgium for some years now.
11 The products left our factory last week.
12 We received them in good condition the day before yesterday.
13 The goods reached our customer this morning.
14 Our agents have worked satisfactorily for us for the last six years.
15 We have spent too much money on market research in recent years.

Übung 16

1 have offered, did
2 has given, gave
3 changed, brought in
4 have, started
5 has been, travelled
6 has, decided
7 have added, agreed
8 have, changed

Übung 17

3 b, 4 a
5 a, 6 b
7 b, 8 a
9 a, 10 b
11 a, 12 b
13 b, 14 a
15 a, 16 b

Übung 18

1 always keep *oder* have always kept
2 has just joined
3 controls
4 have marketed
   oder have been marketing
5 have taken
6 have never had
7 entered
8 was
9 has got damp
10 bought, have not bought
11 has proved
12 use
13 have had
14 called
15 was, was sorting
16 put oder have put
17 were preparing
18 have adopted
19 heard *oder* have heard
20 have worked
   oder have been working
21 has to
22 decides *oder* has decided
23 are looking, have not been
24 are taking up

5 Die Konditionalsätze (if-Sätze)

Übung 1
1 If you read the instructions, you will know ...
2 If we had published regular newsletters for our employees, they would have been ...
3 If you were a computer expert, you would have ...
4 If you passed the entrance examination, you would be able to register ...
5 If they had modernized their equipment, I would have stayed ...
6 If companies installed video-conferencing facilities, it would allow ...
7 If you had been the cheapest supplier, you would have got ...
8 If you work hard, you will get ...
9 If you had had good references, you would have got ...
10 If you speak English fluently, you will get ...
11 If I had got a good offer, I would have accepted ...
12 If I had better computer skills, I would apply ...
13 If microcomputers were built into credit cards, it would revolutionize ...
14 If we had had more open discussions, we would have avoided ...
15 If we had had better management/ staff relations, it would have increased motivation and improved ...

Übung 2
1 If the pattern has ..., we will place ...
   If the pattern had ..., we would place ...
2 If you send ..., we will test ...
   If you had sent ..., we would have tested ...
3 If we were not ..., there would not be ...
   If we had not been ..., there would not have been ...
4 If there were ..., work would be ...
   If there had been ..., work would have been ...
5 He would not leave ... if promotion prospects improved.
   He would not have left ... if promotion prospects had improved.
6 If the company employs ..., it will probably benefit ...
   If the company had employed ..., it would probably have benefitted ...
7 If he had ..., he would get ...
   If he had had ..., he would have got ...
8 If they have ..., their business will improve.
   If they had had ..., their business would have improved.
9 He will be ... if he adopts ...
   He would have been ... if he had adopted ...
10 We will take ... if she applies ...
    We would take ... if she applied ...
11 If you wrote ..., the letter would be delivered ...
    If you had written ..., the letter would have been delivered ...
12 If they send ..., they will not receive ...
    If they sent ..., they would not receive ...

Übung 3
1 will book, have/would book, had/would have booked, had had
2 are, will place/were, would place/had been, would have placed
3 sells, will increase/sold, would increase/had sold, would have increased
4 will not lose, keep/would not lose, kept/would not have lost, had kept
5 will tell, have/would tell, had/would have told, had had

6 will find, run through/would find, ran through/would have found, had run through
7 wants, will need/wanted, would need/had wanted, would have needed
8 will save, arrange/would save, arranged/would have saved, had arranged
9 want, will be/wanted, would be/had wanted, would have been
10 comes up, will tell/came up, would tell/had come up, would have told

Übung 4
1 had passed
2 would have contacted
3 would have re-ordered
4 had been
5 would have done
6 had not met
7 would not have given up
8 would not have got
9 had broadcast
10 would have finished
11 would not have caught
12 had given

Übung 5
1 would choose
2 do not (don't) provide
3 would have taken
4 prove
5 were not
6 will change
7 would save
8 will place
9 would not (wouldn't) have kept
10 had talked
11 would have called
12 would happen
13 will get
14 would be

Übung 6
1 If we had not kept ..., they would not have continued ...
2 If the company had not provided ..., it would not have earned ...
3 If he had not often been ..., they would not have checked ...
4 If we had not been ..., we would not have got ...
5 If we had not studied ..., we would not have learned ...
6 If I had not shown ..., he would not have granted ...
7 If they had not worked ..., they would not have sorted out ...
8 If the new boss had not set ..., the company would not have beaten ...
9 If she had not selected ..., she would not have found ...
10 If they had not set up ..., they would not have identified ...
11 If we had not advertised ..., we would not have had ...
12 If the stockmarket had not been behaving ..., I would not have sold ...
13 If the machines had not been serviced ..., they would not have performed ...
14 If the fog at Heathrow had not been ..., the plane would not have been ...

Übung 7
1 If I was (were) you, I would write ...
2 If I was (were) you, I would look ...
3 If I was (were) you, I would try ...
4 If I was (were) you, I would just ask ...
5 If I was (were) you, I would rethink ...
6 If I was (were) you, I would place ...
7 If I was (were) you, I would have ...
8 If I was (were) you, I would ask ...
9 If I was (were) you, I would tell ...
10 If I was (were) you, I would not rent ...
11 If I was (were) you, I would just go ...
12 If I was (were) you, I would look ...
13 If I was (were) you, I would open ...
14 If I was (were) you, I would install ...
15 If I was (were) you, I would go ...

Übung 8

1. would be
2. does not increase
3. had not renegotiated
4. is
5. decided
6. would have been
7. set up
8. do not do
9. would have lost
10. would be

Übung 9

1. could have finished
2. cannot find
3. must get
4. cannot do
5. may not go
6. must replace
7. must be prepared
8. cannot have
9. must advertise
10. could stop
11. may go
12. could beat
13. must extend
14. could have dealt
15. must send
16. could have exchanged

Übung 10

1. were finished
2. would have been lost
3. had been appointed
4. must be worn
5. will be made
6. had been agreed upon
7. could be issued
8. would be lost
9. will be selected
10. will be asked
11. were asked
12. would be invested

Übung 11

1. have
2. will be reduced
3. will be covered
4. would contact
5. will be asked
6. do not tell
7. would not accept
8. must read
9. did not pay
10. must fill in

6 Die modalen Hilfsverben

Übung 1
1. Everybody will be able to fill in ...
   Everybody has been able to fill in ...
2. You were not able to despatch ...
   You would not have been able to despatch ...
3. We will be able to buy ...
   We would have been able to buy ...
4. We will be able to clear up ...
5. They have not been able to afford ...
   They would not be able to afford ...
6. He would be able to get ...
   He had been able to get ...
7. They were able to increase ...
8. we have not been able to keep up ...
9. We had not been able to ship ...
10. We were not able to develop ...

Übung 2
1. can *oder* will be able to
2. can *oder* are able to
3. could *oder* was able to
4. could *oder* were able to
5. could have paid
   oder would have been able to pay
6. could *oder* would be able to
7. can *oder* are able to
8. can *oder* are able to

Übung 3
1. He will not be allowed to take over ...
2. He was not allowed to drink ...
3. They were not allowed to copy ...
   They have not been allowed to copy ...
4. I would (should) be allowed to rent ...
5. We will not be allowed to cooperate ...
6. They are not allowed to export ...
   They have not been allowed to export ...
7. You would not be allowed to withdraw ...
8. You will not be allowed to deliver ...
9. They would (should) not have been allowed to sell ...
   They are not allowed to sell ...
10. We were not allowed to advertise ...
    We had not been allowed to advertise ...

Übung 4
1. must not
2. may *oder* might
3. may *oder* might
4. must not *oder* are not allowed to
5. must not *oder* are not allowed to
6. may
7. must not *oder* is not allowed to
8. must not *oder* is not allowed to
9. must not *oder* is not allowed to
10. must not *oder* are not allowed to

Übung 5
1. may not
2. could not
3. can *oder* could
4. can
5. can
6. may
7. are not able to
   oder have not been able to
8. might not
9. could not
10. can

Übung 6
1. We had to agree ...
2. He would have to notify ...
3. I will have to type ...
4. They will have to make ...
5. We will have to come ...
6. They had to overcome ...
7. He would have to give up ...
8. They will have to use ...
9. Working conditions on the shop floor had to be ...

10 You will have to aim …
11 We had to attach …
12 The information sheet had to be …
13 We would have to translate …
14 The postcode has to be …

Übung 7

1 a	4 a	7 b	10 a
2 b	5 c	8 a	
3 c	6 a	9 c	

Übung 8

1 No, we needn't./No, we don't need to./No, we don't have to.
2 No, I (you) needn't./No, I (you) don't need to./No, I (you) don't have to.
3 No, they needn't./No, they don't need to./No, they don't have to.
4 No, we needn't./No, we don't need to./No, we don't have to.
5 No, I (you) needn't./No, I (you) don't need to./No, I (you) don't have to.
6 No, they needn't./No, they don't need to./No, they don't have to.
7 No, we needn't./No, we don't need to./No, we don't have to.
8 No, they needn't./No, they don't need to./No, they don't have to.
9 No, we needn't./No, we don't need to./No, we don't have to.
10 No, you needn't./No, you don't need to./No, you don't have to.

Übung 9

1 I will not (won't) have to work …
2 We would not (wouldn't) have to buy …
3 Mrs Jenkins will not (won't) have to fly …
4 They did not (didn't) have to settle …
5 He does not (doesn't) have to attend …
6 They will not (won't) have to confirm …
7 We did not (didn't) have to take …
8 They do not (don't) have to pay …

Übung 10

1 did not have to spend
2 did not have to write
3 need not have made
4 did not have to complete
5 need not have paid
6 need not have told
   oder did not have to tell
7 need not have worried
8 did not have to change
9 need not have tried
10 did not have to pay
11 need not have hurried
   oder did not have to hurry
12 need not have sent
   oder did not have to send
13 did not have to pay
14 need not have sent
15 did not have to worry

Übung 11

1 must not		9 must not
2 must not		10 need not
3 need not		11 need not
4 need not		12 must not
5 must not		13 must not
6 need not		14 need not
7 need not		15 must not
8 must not			

Übung 12

1 Do we have to keep all their letters?
2 Will he have to order new stationery?
3 Do we have to accept foreign coins?
4 Does she have to translate the quotations?
5 Do you have to be late?
6 Did we have to pay compensation?
7 Does he have to complain so much?
8 Did he have to repair the coffee machine?
9 Will they have to wait outside?
10 Do we have to ask for a pay rise?
11 Did we have to cancel the agreement?
12 Will they have to replace the calculators?

Übung 13
1. We should not underestimate ...
2. Shall I take part ...?
3. Should we introduce ...?
   oder Ought we to introduce ...?
4. And am I supposed to do ...?
5. They should have come ...
6. The security guards are supposed to check ...
   oder The security guards should check ...
7. Shall we ask them ...?
8. We should have ...
   oder We ought to have ...
9. Shall I meet ...?
10. Trade Unions are supposed to support ...
    oder Trade Unions should support ...

Übung 14
1. shall
2. should *oder* ought to
3. should
4. Should *oder* Shall
5. should *oder* ought to
6. should
7. should *oder* are supposed to
8. should *oder* ought to
9. should have *oder* ought to have
10. should *oder* are always supposed to

Übung 15
1. should *oder* are supposed to
2. should *oder* are supposed to
3. is said to
4. is supposed to
5. is supposed to
6. should
7. is said to
8. should
9. should *oder* are supposed to

Übung 16
1. intend *oder* mean
2. wish
3. want
4. want
5. are willing
6. intend *oder* mean
7. want
8. is willing
9. want
10. intend *oder* mean
11. wish
12. are willing
13. want
14. wished
15. did not intend *oder* did not mean
16. want
17. intend *oder* mean
18. intends *oder* means

Übung 17
1. should *oder* ought to
2. Yes, you may.
3. wish
4. must *oder* have to
5. will have to
6. may *oder* is allowed to
7. must not *oder* is not allowed to
8. do not intend to *oder* do not mean to
9. cannot
10. could not *oder* were not able to
11. must not *oder* are not allowed to
12. should *oder* ought to
13. want, must *oder* have to
14. must *oder* has to
15. had to
16. should *oder* ought to
17. Might *oder* Could
18. must *oder* have to
19. could
20. must *oder* have to
21. wanted
22. might *oder* could
23. would have to
24. will have to
25. might *oder* could
26. must *oder* have to
27. intended *oder* meant
28. should *oder* ought to

7 Das Gerundium

Übung 1
1. Listening to her is ...
2. Trying it again is ...
3. Starting a new sales campaign at this time of year is ...
4. Taking out a loan with interest rates as high as 15% is ...
5. Sending these goods by ship is ...
6. Admitting a mistake is ...
7. Disregarding safety regulations is ...
8. Sending a letter without a complimentary close is ...
9. Seeing the work-force reduced is ...
10. Having an instruction manual with too many cross-references in it is ...
11. Working in an office without any windows is ...
12. Operating a telex machine used to be ...
13. Faxing a letter is ...
14. Replacing an employee who is lazy is ...
15. Seeing the sales increase after an advertising campaign is ...

Übung 2
1. It is not worthwhile setting up ...
2. It is not worthwhile investing ...
3. It is a pleasure watching (to watch) ...
4. It is not much use sending ...
5. It is no use apologizing ...
6. It is hard accepting (to accept) ...
7. It is no use asking ...
8. She said it was fun speculating (to speculate) ...
9. It is hard repaying (to repay) ...
10. It is hard working (to work) ...
11. It's worthwhile working ...
12. It's no use feeling ...

Übung 3
1. We will keep on sending ...
2. She is practising writing ...
3. We are considering taking ...
4. I think we can justify offering ...
5. Since the introduction of computers we have given up sending ... payments.
6. We must stop granting ... discount.
7. We cannot avoid being ...
8. We cannot risk losing ...
9. Avoid being over-dramatic if ...
10. "I don't mind waiting ..."

Übung 4
1. filing
2. getting
3. studying
4. being made redundant
5. being an expert
6. working on the draft contract
7. not being flexible
8. being selected
9. being involved
10. being too sensitive

Übung 5
1. He (she) is accused of stealing.
2. He (she) concentrates on getting ...
3. They are famous for producing ...
4. They spent all the money on advertising ...
5. They dream of getting ...
6. He (she) objects to working ...
7. He (she) has experience in handling ...
8. He (she) is far from giving up.
9. He (she) is engaged in preparing ...
10. We are incapable of granting ...
11. He has trouble in finding ...
12. She is very clever at finding ...

Übung 6
1. d   in danger of being pushed out
2. c   succeeded in merging with
3. j   far from giving up

4	g	chance of winning
5	f	keen on beating
6	e	delighted about getting
7	b	enthusiastic about working
8	i	possibility of going
9	a	look forward to receiving
10	h	incapable of admitting

Übung 7
1. on having
2. of being
3. for checking
4. to cooperating
5. up complaining
6. of meeting
7. of writing
8. about moving
9. to meeting
10. about losing

Übung 8
(Vor-oder Nachstellung des Adverbialsatzes ist möglich)
1. After landing at Heathrow, they went ...
2. We got the order by making ...
3. He put down the receiver without apologizing.
4. She has not reached the sales target since getting ...
5. They profited from our generous discount scheme by agreeing ...
6. He was removed from the team for being ...
7. You have to finish all your sales calls before chasing up ...
8. She got very angry on hearing ...
9. They delivered all the parcels in spite of being ...
10. By always offering help if anybody has a problem, he has become ...

Übung 9
1. Before buying something on hire purchase, you ...
2. After learning the selling price, ask ...
3. In spite of knowing the rate of interest, you ...
4. Without having (got) all the details, you ...
5. By using a clock card, a worker ...
6. By taking the times stamped on the card, a wages clerk ...
7. By subtracting the normal daily working hours from the hours actually worked, he ...
8. After finding that they actually needed more money than they had, they ...

Übung 10
1. She does not mind the girls smoking ...
2. Do you remember this man applying ...
3. I cannot understand our attorney not answering ...
4. The team strongly dislikes the foreman being ...
5. He dislikes our customers asking ...
6. They were afraid of the Trade Minister raising ...
7. We objected to the personnel manager giving away ...
8. Nobody likes the idea of Miss Wood leaving ...
9. We dislike our supplier making ...
10. We do not mind our night watchmen having ...
11. I'm afraid of the main speaker being ...
12. She hates her trainees being ...

Übung 11
1. You cannot accuse her of being ...
2. You can depend on getting ...
3. The new salesman is very proud of getting (having got) ...
4. She is proud of working ...
5. Do you remember her asking you ...
6. I don't mind them selling ...
7. Mr Reade is fond of visiting ...
8. She could not help laughing at ...
9. They got a prize for exceeding ...
10. I object to her being removed (having been removed) ...

8 Das Partizip

Übung 1
1. smiling
2. smoking
3. drinking
4. eating
5. sleeping
6. protesting
7. grumbling
8. complaining
9. listening

Übung 2
1. give *oder* giving
2. take
3. repairing
4. playing
5. unplug
6. reading
7. bang
8. warning
9. arguing
10. being
11. knock
12. reporting
13. put *oder* putting
14. coming
15. enter, pass, go, rush, sit

Übung 3
1. heard her talking
2. saw it working
3. saw her leave smiling
4. saw her turn pale
5. heard him being
6. saw her sign
7. hear them talking
8. hear something bubbling
9. saw him drop it
10. heard it fall and break
11. saw him grab, put out
12. heard Susan ordering

Übung 4
1. waiting
2. sealed
3. replaced
4. standing
5. serviced
6. checked
7. working
8. exchanged

Übung 5
1. have
2. kept
3. have
4. left
5. had
6. have
7. keep *oder* kept
8. had
9. left *oder* kept
10. had

Übung 6
1. distributed
2. labelled
3. cut
4. looking
5. reimbursed
6. sorting
7. waiting
8. replaced

Übung 7
1. The management meeting taking place this afternoon ...
2. The suggestions made at the meeting ...
3. The advertisement published in the national newspapers ...
4. A company not offering sufficient opportunities ...
5. A company showing a caring attitude ...
6. Candidates applying for higher management positions ...
7. A company not having a fair promotion system ...
8. The assessment department established two years ago ...
9. Executives criticizing our assessment department ...
10. A group of countries having no internal tariff barriers ...
11. ... the Council of Ministers made up of government ministers ...
12. Representatives sitting in the European Parliament ...
13. The body running the day to day business ...
14. ... the institution dealing with governments ...

Übung 8

1 Coming into his office next morning, Mr Reade found ...
2 Feeling hungry, they both went ...
3 Having worked hard all day, they felt ...
4 Having finished the letter, she had...
5 Feeling ill, she could ...
6 Never having worked for a big company before, Penny felt ...
7 Not wanting to admit his mistake, he paid ...
8 Having lost the requisition form, he had to ...
9 Having been refused an import licence, we had to ...
10 Having discussed prices again, they were able ...
11 Having forgotten the departure time, she was ...
12 Not quite understanding (having understood) some of the terms, they had to ...
13 Having worked on the development of the new system, she was asked ...
14 Having carried out a survey of our employees' attitudes to their jobs, we can ...
15 Not having been promoted last year, she did not work ...

Übung 9

1 Having passed the examination, she applied ...
2 Exchanging the blades of the shredder, he got ...
3 Putting out his cigarette, he entered ...
4 Having managed to do it alone, the apprentices proudly showed ...
5 Reading the job advertisements eagerly, Sam hoped ...
   oder Hoping for a stroke of luck, Sam read ...
6 Having found the reason for the breakdown, they repaired ...
7 Having worked for a similar company before, she overcame ...
8 (Having been) Installed and connected last month, the machine has worked ...
9 Having both been sacked, they joined ...
10 Tripping over the carpet, he dropped ...
11 Hoping to go before the selection board, he improved ...
12 Accused of not meeting the deadline, our suppliers had to ...

Übung 10

1 unless
2 By
3 Although
4 If
5 Until
6 If
7 Although
8 unless
9 while
10 By

Übung 11

1 With the go-ahead given by the Board ...
2 With a lot of pickets standing at the gate ...
3 With the shortlist finished ...
4 With the number of car thefts rising sharply ...
5 With company cars now being taxed ...
6 With the blinds removed ...
7 With import taxes being raised ...
8 With many young people intending to be bankers ...
9 With demand falling and all our costs increasing ...
10 With Rix Ltd. starting a new sales campaign ...

Übung 12

1 His commission having been raised considerably, Charles ...
2 We could hear them arguing ...
3 After taking into account all possible options, he decided ...
4 With the old SX model no longer

draining our budget, we could ...
5 No worker will be satisfied unless given ...
6 Not willing to wait for an answer, she asked ...
7 Before going home, they wanted ...
8 If asked, don't tell ...
9 By being indecisive, our salesman lost ...
10 Having been overlooked when it came to promotion, the foreman left ...
11 After being thoroughly trained for their new job, their probation period was ...
12 With their working capital adapted to the company's needs, their financial position seems ...
13 Since joining this company, I have ...
14 He saw the receptionist making ...
15 Often criticized for being late, he always had ...
16 Having put the finishing touches to the new office building, they could ...
17 Time permitting, we shall ...
18 He saw Mr Reade driving ...
19 Before collecting all the available information, the Chairman expressed ...
20 Having arrived at the conclusion that we must reduce our costs by 10%, he cancelled ...

9 Der Infinitiv

Übung 1
1. She was clever enough to pass ...
2. Mrs Jenkins was too angry to talk ...
3. Our chief buyer is sensible enough not to accept ...
4. We are too busy to have ...
5. The box is too bulky to be sent ...
6. He was too excited to answer ...
7. At last he said he had enough money to buy ...
8. The profit was not big enough to get ...
9. The lorry was not big enough to take ...
10. Penny is not tall enough to reach ...

Übung 2
1. Bill was the last to leave ...
2. There was not a single person to help ...
3. When stopped at the gate he had nothing to use ...
4. Our department was the first to finish ...
5. She would have been the first to admit ...
6. Only Tom did not see anything to laugh ...
7. It was the worst thing to happen ...
8. Their order is the next to be ...
9. Helen was the first woman to become ...
10. The *Financial Times* is the best paper to read ...

Übung 3
1. She wondered what to say ...
2. Tom had better learn when to wear ...
3. Do you know how to get ...
4. Mr Reade didn't know whether to smile ...
5. We do not yet know who to invite ...
6. She knows very well how to settle ...
7. We did not know what to do ...
8. I do not know whether to maintain ...
9. He did not know where to ask ...
10. They were not sure whether to submit ...

Übung 4
1. I don't want you to interrupt ...
2. I expect her to photocopy ...
3. I want them only to send ...
4. I told Tom to deliver ...
5. I advise you to buy ...
6. We expect you to arrange ...
7. I advised him not to believe ...
8. I want her to control ...
9. I told them to find out ...
10. I don't want this company to lose ...
11. I advised him to reconsider ...
12. I want you only to buy ...

Übung 5
1. I would like you to come and see ...
2. They replied that we had ...
3. We told them that we had not received ...
4. They want us to send ...
5. We urged them to deliver ...
6. She told us to be more precise ...
7. We hope that they will give us ...
8. They advised us to advertise ...

Übung 6
1. ... for them to complain before replacing the faulty items.
2. ... for him to go alone on his first trip abroad.
3. ... for you to study in the plane.
4. ... for our workers to lift.
5. ... for Penny to work at the reception desk because she knows a lot of people.

6 ... for him to polish up his Italian.
7 ... for them to first learn something about management structures.
8 ... for me to go to the bank now.

Übung 7

1 give
2 alter
3 go
4 to give
5 wait
6 translate
7 to come back, stay
8 to know
9 look
10 to attend
11 to come
12 to do
13 go
14 pick up, take
15 promise to avoid
16 be
17 stay
18 to send

Übung 8

1 to lower
2 accept
3 keep
4 to send
5 give
6 buy
7 to express
8 arrange
9 smile
10 see
11 to observe
12 drop
13 to panic
14 to park
15 to meet
16 wait
17 to arrive
18 to remove
19 pay
20 go
21 to stop
22 leave
23 steal
24 retype

Übung 9

1 No, he was too shy to.
2 I told you to.
3 He wanted to but ...
4 You were told not to.
5 Yes, I plan to if ...
6 I meant to but ...
7 I know she used to but ...
8 She had to because ...
9 She used to when ...
10 I know, I am just going to.